P9-CSB-533

The School for Husbands

AND

The Imaginary Cuckold,
or Sganarelle

The School for Husbands
AND
The Imaginary Cuckold, or Sganarelle

By Molière

Translated into English verse
by Richard Wilbur

THEATRE COMMUNICATIONS GROUP
NEW YORK
2009

The School for Husbands and *The Imaginary Cuckold, or Sganarelle* are
copyright © 1992, 1993, 2009 by Richard Wilbur

Foreword is copyright © 2009 by John Simon

The School for Husbands and *The Imaginary Cuckold, or Sganarelle* are published by
Theatre Communications Group, Inc., 520 Eighth Avenue, 24th Floor,
New York, NY 10018–4156

Reprinted by special arrangement with Houghton Mifflin Harcourt Publishing
Company.

All rights reserved. Except for brief passages quoted in newspaper, magazine, radio
or television reviews, no part of this book may be reproduced in any form or by any
means, electronic or mechanical, including photocopying or recording, or by an information storage and retrieval system, without permission in writing from the publisher.

Professionals and amateurs are hereby warned that this material, being fully
protected under the Copyright Laws of the United States of America and all other
countries of the Berne and Universal Copyright Conventions, is subject to a roy-
alty. All rights including, but not limited to, professional, amateur, recording, motion
picture, recitation, lecturing, public reading, radio and television broadcasting, and
the rights of translation into foreign languages are expressly reserved. Particular
emphasis is placed on the question of readings and all uses of this book by educa-
tional institutions, permission for which must be secured from the author's repre-
sentative: Peter Franklin, William Morris Agency, 1325 Avenue of the Americas,
15th Floor, New York, NY 10019, 212-586-5100.

This project is funded by the Sidney E. Frank Foundation.

This publication is made possible in part with public funds from the New York
State Council on the Arts, a State Agency.

TCG books are exclusively distributed to the book trade by Consortium Book
Sales and Distribution.

LIBRARY OF CONGRESS CATALOGING-IN-PUBLICATION DATA
Molière, 1622–1673.
[Ecole des maris. English]
The school for husbands ; The imaginary cuckold, or, Sganarelle / by Molière ;
translated into English verse by Richard Wilbur.—1st ed.
p. cm.
ISBN 978-1-55936-338-9
I. Molière, 1622–1673—Translations into English. I. Wilbur, Richard, 1921–
II. Molière, 1622–1673. Sganarelle, ou, Le cocu imaginaire. English. III. Title.
IV. Title: Imaginary cuckold, or, Sganarelle. V. Title: Imaginary cuckold. VI.
Title: Sganarelle.
PQ1825.E5W5   2009
842'.4—dc22   2009016305

Cover design by Chip Kidd
Cover image: Burstein Collection/Corbis
Text design and composition by Lisa Govan

First Edition, May 2009

For Brian Bedford

Contents

Foreword

By John Simon

Literary trends come and go, and yesterday's favorite may be forgotten tomorrow. But most nations have one supreme author—poet, playwright or novelist—who is the fountainhead of their literature. For England, it is Shakespeare; for Germany, Goethe; for Italy, Dante.

For France, this role is shared by two superstars: the great tragedian Racine, and the great comedian Molière. Racine stands for purity, a classically restrained vocabulary of great musicality; Molière, whose motto was, "I gather my property where I find it," offers profusion of motley mirth.

Most of Molière's greatest dramatic achievements are in rhymed verse, in the traditional French alexandrine, a rhymed, regular, twelve-syllable line. English verse drama, unlike French, is in an accented language and traditionally espouses the five-beat pentameter line of slightly varied length. It avoids being as regimented as the unaccentual French, lest the monotonously placed drumbeats produce doggerel. The wonder of it is that Wilbur's translations attain all the lightly tripping elegance of the originals.

It should be noted that Wilbur is one of our finest poets, but also one of the best—perhaps the best—verse translators into English. As a poet, he has won all possible prizes, but he deserves as many as translator, not only of the verse plays of Molière and Racine, but also of lyrics from various languages. The translations contained in this volume—*The School for Husbands* and *The Imaginary Cuckold, or Sganarelle*—should provide ample proof.

Consider, for example, Wilbur's masterly use of enjambment—run-on lines taboo in the strictly end-stopped French—to excellent effect. Take this enjambed couplet, "My name's no longer Sganarelle, and folk / Will dub me Mister Staghorn, for a joke." The enjambment both slightly downplays the rhyme and creates a certain suspense: Just what will folk do? It has been argued, that there is some loss of "darkness" in the translations, to which Wilbur replies, in his collection of prose pieces *The Catbird's Song*, "English rhyming is more emphatic than French rhyming, so that a translation into English couplets will more often have the whip-crack sound of joke or epigram than the original did."

That is a consequence of an accentual language, but, in my view, neither decreases nor increases whatever is meant by "darkness." What is true and important about the couplets in both French and English is that they add musicality while also acting as a mnemonic aid by making consecutive lines click satisfyingly and memorably into place. They also challenge the actor to the bravura feat of neither emphasizing nor wholly losing the rhyme—or, otherwise put, to reconcile naturalness and artifice.

There exists a centuries-old toy the French call *bilboquet* and we call cup and ball. A wooden ball is attached by a fairly extensive string to a long-handled wooden cup; when the ball is propelled into the air, it must be caught by the cup into which it snugly fits. So, too, Wilbur's couplets, in which there are no awkward inversions, omissions, flab or obscurities. You might say they snap to.

Some examples from *Cuckold*. Sganarelle's wife, of her husband: "He saves his hugs for other women, the swine, / And feeds their appetites while starving mine." And he, jealously, to her: "Why, when your mate's well favored, spry and dapper, / Were you attracted to this whippersnapper?" The maid, to her mistress, Célie, as they look at the locket picture of her would-be lover, Lélie: "He has a faithful lover's face, that's true, / And you're quite right to love him as you do."

Note the monosyllabic, so-called masculine swine-mine rhyme, and the feminine dapper-whippersnapper rhyme handled with equal easefulness, with the utterance perfectly fitted to the characters and situations—everyday language suited to bourgeois speakers and their savvy servants. How aptly the rhymes fall where they do—like the ball into the *bilboquet*—allowing you to subliminally sense the rhyming without dwelling on it consciously, and so impede the smooth flow of the dialogue.

Now let us take stock of Molière's artful construction of the farce in *Cuckold,* while noting how that entire play, like much of *Husbands*, revolves around cuckoldry, whether real or imagined. Cuckoldry is a principal topic of the Italian commedia dell'arte, the traditional clown shows that so much of contemporaneous French farce and early Molière imitated.

Why, we may ask, is this subject all over romance-language theater, whereas, of all Shakespeare's plays, featured only in *Othello* and less prominently in *Cymbeline* and *The Winter's Tale*? Because in Latin countries, at least in prefeminist times, though a husband was allowed a mistress, absolute faithfulness of the wife was a must. Consequently, the metaphoric horns of the husband, real or merely suspected, become a prime subject of both comedy and tragedy, whether as laughing matter or as cause of bloodshed.

A farce such as *Cuckold* depends entirely on plot and language: The characters are as stock as can be: The typical older, bamboozled husband; the typical young lover and married or unmarried—but closely guarded or promised to another—beloved; the typical blustering and draconian father; the typical cunning or rascally servants; and, of course, misunderstandings galore on the way to a glibly contrived happy ending.

But look how especially intricate the imbroglio is in *Cuckold*, thanks to nothing much more than Célie's locket found by the wife of the jealous Sganarelle, a little courtesy of his to the fainting Célie, and the wife's Samaritan kindness to the crushed Lélie, who mistakenly assumes Célie to have married Sganarelle. There is a kind of geometry to this that a mathematician could diagram, and it takes a maid's arbitrary common sense and a potential rival's clandestine previous marriage for the facile disentangling of knots.

What delights is the way one misapprehension dovetails into another, and also the vengeance-bent Sganarelle's cowardly tergiversations couched in soliloquy worthy of some tragic hero. Further, the comical quarrels between Sganarelle and wife, and between Lélie and Célie, whose very rhyming names contribute to the comic absurdity.

There is, clearly, no allowance for the characters to have a certain density beyond serving as instruments of the plot. In *The School for Husbands* some greater individualization appears, though still a long way short of that in the later masterpieces.

Between this 1660 farce and the 1661 comedy, the difference does not affect plot. The story is still arrantly contrived. A dying man bequeathed his little daughters to a pair of brothers, his friends, for rearing and, presumably, eventual marrying. Léonor was given to Ariste, now sixtyish; Isabelle to Sganarelle, now forty. Isabelle, kept on a leash by despotic Sganarelle, has fallen in love with young Valère, who has been trailing her and has elicited an exchange of amorous glances. Léonor, whom the wise Ariste brought up tolerantly, is devoted to him. There is thus a sense of how a liberal character begets affection, while a domineering one elicits rebellion.

Here an autobiographical element enters. In the prime French edition of Molière's oeuvre, the two volumes in the Pléiade series, the editor, Maurice Rat, gives a detailed account of a major controversy that seems to have no resolution.

The beautiful redheaded leading lady of Molière's company, Madeleine Béjart, besides having some aristocratic sugar-daddies also indulged in more fleeting affairs, one of them with Molière himself. Because some key documents are rather suspiciously missing, it is to this day debated whether the eighteen- or nineteen-year-old Armande Béjart, likewise an actress in the company, was Madeleine's younger sister or illegitimate daughter. When the forty-year-old playwright married her in 1662, his numerous envious enemies rumored that he was in fact her father—given Madeleine's lifestyle, not impossible.

In any case, the marriage was a troubled one, what with Armande, too, being an innocent or not-so-innocent flirt (like Célimène in *The Misanthrope*, modeled on and acted by her), and the spousal quarrels and frequent separations.

It seems to me more than likely that by the year of writing *The School for Husbands,* and thus less than a year before their marriage, Molière was already doting on the pert Armande, and worriedly contemplating marrying her. This would then translate into the forty-year-old Sganarelle's jealousy of Isabelle, just as Ariste's good treatment of Léonor, played by Armande, would have been a preemptive strategy in the hope that the character's decency would rub off on the interpreter.

The success of *The Imaginary Cuckold, or Sganarelle* was considerable, both in the city and, later, at court. With Molière, dressed in red from top to toe as Sganarelle, it achieved altogether 122 performances, not bad for its time. It also marked the first appearance of the character Sganarelle, whom Molière resuscitated in four more plays in somewhat different guises, but always in some manner louche. However grotesque, though, he remains, as has been duly observed, ever human enough.

Curiously, Rat writes that "one must concede that [Molière's] principal merit is not as a versifier, and that all too often he manages rhyme only with the aid of fillers or, at the very least, by small, rather annoying deviations." And Wilbur corroborates, "He wasn't really a poet outside of the plays, and inside the poetic plays he's a very prosaic poet in many respects."

I myself am not bothered by any of this, either in the French originals or in Wilbur's masterly translations. To the degree that the problem exists, it contributes to the earthy realism of the plays. But let me quote here the opinions of four major men of letters on Molière.

Paul Valéry—master poet, dramatist, philosopher and critic— wrote: "Molière has largely contributed to basing the French theater on cuckoldry and low elements; by genius, he sanctioned ignoble farces; he gave, through several masterpieces, an authority one may marvel at to the most commonplace things. He set the laughers, which is to say the average, against the exceptional— or, rather, he situated himself among this average." That is the elitist view.

Now for Ferdinand Brunetière, one of the most influential nineteeth-century literary historians and critics: "Molière is of the family of Rabelais and Voltaire, like them a free spirit, independent in mood, pagan like them, if you will, and like them adherent of the cult of nature and humanity. [His targets] are all those of whom it may be said that their ridiculousness or odiousness consists essentially of cosmeticizing, disguising, masking or denaturing nature." That is the practicing critic's view.

Next, here is Hugo von Hofmannsthal, the great Austrian poet, playwright, librettist and essayist, who found Molière "capable of producing a discourse flexible and fiery enough to switch around the earth and the heavens; to think up figures and put speeches in their mouths issuing as naturally from them as the meow from a cat; with a wit that tickled the midriff while at the same time making the heart beat faster or slower, and checking in higher up at the brow to awaken human understanding." This is the enthusiast's view.

Finally, the words of Sacha Guitry, a jewel of the twentieth-century French theater as writer, director and performer: "He aimed at making people think without letting them know that he was doing so." The view of the practical man of the theater, well aware of the public's unease with ideas.

It is to be hoped that the reader will not stop at these early works, fun as they are, but pursue his exploration of Molière to a number of his remarkable further plays, culminating in two of the world theater's highest peaks: *Tartuffe* and *The Misanthrope*. And this, if not in the French, then in Richard Wilbur's translations, which are, in that useful German word lacking in our language, *kongenial*—meaning not, as in English, congenial, but something bigger: equal in genius.

New York
April 2009

The School for Husbands

Introduction

Molière was devotedly familiar, all his life, with the *commedia dell'arte,* that form of Italian popular comedy in which stock characters like Pantalone (an amorous old miser) and Arlecchino (a foolish servant) improvised their scenes within skeletal plot outlines or "scenarios." During his thirteen years of touring in the provinces, Molière without question saw and learned from those commedia troupes which, in the seventeenth century, traveled to all of the centers of Europe; and his biographer Grimarest says that the company which he brought to Paris in 1658 was "trained to extemporize short comic pieces in the manner of the Italian actors." When, in that year, he pleased the court with his farce *Le Docteur amoureux,* and secured the patronage of the king's brother, his Troupe de Monsieur was given the use, for half of each week, of the Salle du Petit-Bourbon, sharing that theater with a resident Italian company headed by the great commedia actor Tiberio Fiorelli. Contemporary accounts tell us that it was a happy association, and that Molière never missed one of Fiorelli's performances.

An admiring indebtedness to Italian comedy, outweighing all other influences, can be seen throughout Molière's plays and entertainments, but seems to me particularly visible in his early success *The School for Husbands* (1661). The single setting of the play is that public square, with its clustered houses or "mansions," which was the traditional backdrop of commedia performances. The action recalls the commonest of commedia plots, in which the *innamorati* or young lovers, balked by their elders and aided by clever servants, manage to outwit their oppressors and marry. As for the characters, Sganarelle is one of Molière's quirky Pantalones, and Lisette and Ergaste are French cousins of those *zanni* who, in the Italian comedy, represented impudent servants with a taste for intrigue.

The School for Husbands, however, is a firmly constructed, fully written play in the high mode of verse comedy. Nothing is left to improvisation. Such a farcical bit as Valère and Ergaste's accosting of the oblivious Sganarelle (Act One, Scene 3), which in commedia would give the actors all sorts of inventive latitude, is here wholly worded and choreographed by the dialogue and stage directions. The chief persons of the play, though behind them loom certain stock figures, are variously individuated by Molière's art and endowed with a measure of complexity. In the first act of *Husbands,* we meet two middle-aged brothers, Sganarelle and Ariste, who have promised a dying friend to rear, and perhaps ultimately to marry, his two orphaned daughters. Ariste, an easygoing man of fifty-nine or so, has treated his spirited ward Léonor in a considerate and indulgent fashion, thus gaining her grateful affection. Sganarelle, Ariste's junior by twenty years, is a premature fuddy-duddy who has raised his charge Isabelle with a domineering strictness, and it will of course be the business of the play to rescue her from his tyranny and unite her with her romantic young neighbor Valère. Certain peculiarities of Sganarelle (whose central part was originally played by Molière himself) are conveyed in the play's early scenes: His cranky opposition to fashion and to urban social pleasures, his extolling of ancestral ways and standards, his crusty bad manners, his mistrustfulness, his ill will toward Ariste. All these things, as the second and third acts proceed, become intelligible aspects of his psychology.

As Albert Bermel has noted, the second act—in which the cause of Isabelle is advanced by a series of clever deceptions and dodges—has a number of surprises for us. Isabelle, who in Act One was a poor victim with but twenty-nine syllables to say, emerges in Act Two as a mettlesome, resourceful young woman who, horrified by the prospect of a marriage to a bully, drives all the action by improvising one ruse after another. It is surprising, too, that the enamored Valère and his canny valet Ergaste, who at the end of the first act retired to ponder stratagems, are in the second reactive at best, their behavior being largely confined to the divining of Isabelle's purposes and the abetting of her initiatives. When the figures of a play behave in unexpected and yet credible ways, it increases their dimensionality, and here it is above all the unanticipated actions of Sganarelle which serve to build complex character. The suspicious man of Act One becomes, in Act Two, utterly gullible; the harsh guardian becomes a doting dispenser of pet names; the possessive husband-to-be develops a maudlin sympathy for his young rival. Out of these apparent contradictions we assemble a portrait of an anxious, alienated man, resentful of his brother's sociable aplomb and out of touch with people in general—a man who, significantly, can be blind to others when they are present (Act One, Scene 3) and can fancy them present when they are not. ("Who goes there? Ah, I'm dreaming.") His outlandish views and posturings are intended, we perceive, to confer a style upon his isolation and, as Lionel Gossman says, to impress the world by a claim of superiority to it. In his grandiose insecurity, Sganarelle cannot allow others their freedom and their differences; his relation to the world consists in berating it, and in demanding of others that they regard him as a model and embody his values. It is not, after all, surprising that so shaky and fantastic a man should be disarmed by the feigned docility of Isabelle, and duped by the flatteries of Valère.

But the play, as we experience it, is not always busy with the revelation of personality; it is also, and perhaps more densely, concerned with portraying the intricacies of communication in an atmosphere of intrigue—with suspicion, deception, implication, inference, double entendre, the understanding or misunderstanding of look or word. In the latter part of Act Two, Scene 2, for example, Isabelle has asked Sganarelle to convey an ambiguous message which she intends as a signal to Valère that she is aware of his passion; Sganarelle understands the message as a stern rebuff, and delivers it with an admixture of his own jealous vehemence; Valère does not know what to make of this filtered communication, sent by his beloved but spoken by his rival; Ergaste, however, hypothesizes a secret and favorable meaning, and the departing Sganarelle, looking back at Ergaste and Valère in colloquy, more than once misreads the latter's facial expressions. Given so rich a fabric of doubtful interactions, a critic might well classify *The School for Husbands* as "comedy of intrigue," and many have done so. Others have as firmly called it "comedy of character." Some have treated it as a hybrid transitional piece—an anticipation of deeper character-studies to come, or a sketch for *The School for Wives* (1662), which would return to its theme and rework certain of its situations. Yet it seems to me that we may find this play quite sufficient in its own right, judging with Jacques Guicharnaud that its balance of elements is "esthetically satisfying"; with Donald Frame that it represents Molière's "first demonstration of complete mastery of his craft"; with Martin Turnell that, whatever its place in the canon, it is a "constant delight."

The title of *The School for Husbands* may seem to imply that the play is a lecture, in which the author advocates permissive child-rearing and the laissez-faire treatment of young women and wives. Certainly the comedy appealed to the ladies of Molière's day, whose enthusiasm was a great factor in its success; and as surely there will be those who, presenting it in this translation, will be tempted to give it a strong feminist spin. They will be the more inclined to do so because Ariste, whom some have taken to be Molière's spokesman, is rewarded by the plot with the fond fidelity of Léonor. Still, it is well to remember that the *raisonneurs* of Molière are never effectual or wholly admirable in their arguments, and that their major function is to play straight-man to the aberrated central figure, exacerbating him and prompting him to display his imbalance. It is an impoverishment, furthermore, to treat a dramatic character as a mere mouthpiece, and readers should bear in mind that Ariste's views and actions are conditioned by the desire of an aging man to retain the goodwill of a lively, beautiful young woman. We should also recognize that Isabelle, though driven by circumstances to hoodwink her guardian, is not at all a social rebel. Neither she nor Léonor shares the servants' relish for amorous trickery; she repeatedly asks the audience, in asides or little soliloquies, to excuse her subterfuges; and in her letter to Valère she regrets being forced "to overstep the bounds of decorum prescribed for my sex." There is no question, in *School for Husbands,* as to where our sympathies are to lie, but the play seems less a positive case for specific freedoms than a depiction of oppressive folly. If we look in this work for Molière's "ideas," we can most confidently do so by focusing on Sganarelle: In him, as in the Orgon of *Tartuffe,* we see that it is wrong, and deserving of ridicule, to misuse one's authority as parent or husband, and that—on the comic stage at least, where Nature tends to triumph—such tyranny will bring about its own undoing.

This French play, now three hundred and thirty years old, is like Molière's work generally in requiring little or no mediation; it comes across to us readily, in spite of time and cultural differences. But the reader may be amused by this footnote, which I take from Von Laun's old prose translation, and which has to do with the royal edict brought on stage by Sganarelle at the beginning of Act Two, Scene 6: "It is remarkable that Louis XIV, who was so extravagant himself in his buildings, dress and general expenses, published sixteen laws against luxury; the law Sganarelle speaks of was promulgated November 27th 1660, against the use of *guipures, cannetilles, paillettes,* etc., on men's dresses." Sganarelle's speech, then, is topical; and since it praises the king's decree through the lips of a crank, it may be one of those passages in which Molière felt free to josh his royal or noble patrons with a jester's impunity.

In working on this translation, I have been helped at times by the prose versions of Baker and Miller, of Wall and of Von Laun. My wife, as always, has been my chief consultant. I must also thank Jean Migrenne, William Jay Smith, Sonja Haussmann Smith and Albert Bermel for their clarifications of particular passages, and James Merrill for his kindness in reading the whole.

—RW
Cummington, Massachusetts, 1991

CHARACTERS

SGANARELLE (skan-a-RELL), a man approaching forty; brother to Ariste and guardian to Isabelle

ARISTE (ah-REEST), Sganarelle's elder brother by twenty years; guardian to Léonor

ISABELLE (eez-a-BELL), Léonor's sister, Sganarelle's young ward

LÉONOR (lay-o-NOR), Isabelle's sister, Ariste's ward

LISETTE (lee-ZET), Léonor's maid

VALÈRE (va-LAIR), Isabelle's lover

ERGASTE (air-GHAST), valet to Valère

A MAGISTRATE

A NOTARY

PLACE

The scene throughout: A residential square in Paris.

Act One

Sganarelle, Ariste.

SGANARELLE

Enough talk, Brother; let's give our tongues a rest,
And let's each live his life as he thinks best.
Although you're my superior in age
And old enough, indeed, to be a sage,
Nevertheless I hereby notify you
That I don't care to be corrected by you,
That my own taste suffices to advise me,
And that my way of life quite satisfies me.

ARISTE

Yet all condemn it.

SGANARELLE

Yes, idiots of your sort,
Dear Brother.

ARISTE

Thank you; what a sweet retort!

SGANARELLE

Since you won't drop the subject, tell me, do,
What these fine critics take exception to.

ARISTE

They blame that surly humor which makes you flee
From all the pleasures of society,
And lends a sort of grim outlandishness
To all you do, even to the way you dress.

SGANARELLE

I see: I mustn't wear what clothes I please,
But must submit to fashion's wise decrees!
Do you propose, by precepts so bizarre,
Dear elder Brother—for that is what you are
By twenty blesséd years, I must confess,
Although of course it couldn't matter less—
Do you propose, I say, to force me to
Adorn myself as your young dandies do?
To wear those little hats which leave their brains,
Such as they are, exposed to winds and rains,
And those immense blond wigs which hide their features
And make one doubt that they are human creatures?
Those tiny doublets, cut off at armpit level,
Those collars hanging almost to the navel,
Those sleeves that drag through soups and gravy boats,
And those huge breeches, loose as petticoats?

Those small, beribboned slippers, too neat for words,
Which make them look like feather-footed birds?
Those rolls of lace they force their legs to wear
Like the leg irons that slaves and captives bear,
So that we see each fop and fashion plate
Walk like a pigeon, with a waddling gait?
You'd have me dress like that? I note with loathing
That you're attired in just such modish clothing.

ARISTE

It's best at all times to observe convention
And not, by being odd, attract attention.
For all extremes offend, and wise men teach
Themselves to deal with fashion as with speech,
Accepting calmly, with no fuss or haste,
Whatever changes usage has embraced.
I'm far from recommending those whose passion
Is always to improve upon the fashion,
And who are filled with envy and dismay
If someone else is more extreme than they:
But it is bad, on any ground, to shun
The norm, and not to do the thing that's done;
Better by far to join the foolish throng
Than stand alone and call the whole world wrong.

SGANARELLE

There speaks a vain old man who slyly wears
A black wig to conceal his few white hairs.

ARISTE

It's strange with what persistence and ill grace
You throw my age forever in my face,
And how incessantly I'm forced to hear
You blame my style of dress and my good cheer:

13

As if old age should bid all joys good-bye,
Thinking of nothing save that it must die,
And doesn't look grotesque enough unless
It's sour of mood and dismal in its dress.

SGANARELLE

However that may be, my firm intent
Is not to alter my habiliment.
Despite the mode, I'll have a hat that's made
To shield my head and give my eyes some shade,
A fine long doublet which will wrap me 'round
To warm my belly and keep digestion sound,
Breeches which fit me well in thighs and seat,
And sturdy shoes which won't torment my feet.
Thus did our forebears dress, and they were wise;
Those I offend are free to shut their eyes.

Scene 2

Léonor, Isabelle, Lisette; Ariste and Sganarelle, talking unobserved at the front of the stage.

LÉONOR

(To Isabelle:)
I'll take the blame, if he should make a scene.

LISETTE

(To Isabelle:)
Shut in your lonely room all day? How mean!

ISABELLE

He's like that.

LÉONOR

Sister, I'm sorry for your plight.

LISETTE

(To Léonor:)
His brother and he are just like day and night.
Madam, the Fates were kind in giving you,
As guardian, the sane one of the two.

ISABELLE

I marvel that for one day he should fail
To drag me with him, or shut me in my jail.

LISETTE

I'd send him and his Spanish ruff to Hades,
If—

SGANARELLE

(Lisette having bumped into him:)
    Where are you going, may I ask, young ladies?

LÉONOR

We don't yet know, but since the weather's fair
I've asked my sister out to take the air,
And—

SGANARELLE

(To Léonor:)
    You may go where you like, for all of me.
Just run along.
(Pointing to Lisette:)
        She'll keep you company.
(To Isabelle:)
But you, if you please, won't go on this excursion.

15

ARISTE

Oh, Brother, let them go. They need diversion.

SGANARELLE

Your servant, Brother.

ARISTE

Youth must be permitted—

SGANARELLE

Youth, sir, is foolish; and age can be half-witted.

ARISTE

With Léonor, could she come to any ill?

SGANARELLE

No; but with me she will be safer still.

ARISTE

But—

SGANARELLE

All that she does I strictly oversee,
Thus honoring my responsibility.

ARISTE

And do I neglect her sister, would you say?

SGANARELLE

Well, each man thinks and acts in his own way.
These girls are orphans. Their father, our dear friend,
Entrusted them to us at his life's end,
Bidding us marry them, if so inclined,
Or find them spouses of a proper kind.

Thus we have ruled them with the double sway
Of father and husband, from their childhood's day.
That one, dear Brother, you undertook to rear,
And I took charge of raising this one, here;
Pray govern yours according to your views,
And let me train the other as I choose.

ARISTE

I think—

SGANARELLE

I think, and firmly will declare,
That that's how we should manage this affair.
You let your charge be dashingly arrayed:
So be it; she has a flunky and a maid;
I'm quite content; she idly gads about,
And our young beaux are free to seek her out:
All that is splendid. But my charge, be it known,
Shall live by my desires, and not her own;
She'll dress in serge, in simple browns and grays,
And not wear black except on holidays;
Like any prudent girl, she'll stay indoors
And occupy herself with household chores;
In leisure time she'll mend my linen, or make
Some knitted stockings for amusement's sake;
She'll close her ears to young men's fancy talk,
And never go unguarded for a walk.
The flesh is weak, as each day's gossip warns.
If I can help it, I shall not wear horns,
And since her destiny's to be my wife,
I mean to guard her as I would my life.

ISABELLE

You have no reason—

17

SGANARELLE

Be still. You know you're not
To leave the house without me. Had you forgot?

LÉONOR

Oh, come, sir—

SGANARELLE

Madam, I'd rather not debate
With one whose wit and wisdom are so great.

LÉONOR

Are you vexed to find me here with Isabelle?

SGANARELLE

Why, yes—because you spoil her, truth to tell.
Frankly, your visits here disturb my peace,
And you'd oblige me if they were to cease.

LÉONOR

Well, shall I speak with equal frankness, sir?
I don't know how all this may sit with her,
But such mistrust, I know, would rouse my ire;
And, though we share a mother and a sire,
We're not true sisters if the things you do,
Day after day, can make her fond of you.

LISETTE

Yes, all these stern precautions are inhuman.
Are we in Turkey, where they lock up women?
It's said that females there are slaves or worse,
And that's why Turks are under Heaven's curse.
Our honor, sir, is truly very frail
If we, to keep it, must be kept in jail.
But do you think that such severities

Bar us, in fact, from doing what we please,
Or that, when we're dead set upon some plan,
We can't run rings around the cleverest man?
All these constraints are vain and ludicrous:
The best course, always, is to trust in us.
It's dangerous, sir, to underrate our gender.
Our honor likes to be its own defender.
It almost gives us a desire to sin
When men mount guard on us and lock us in,
And if my husband were so prone to doubt me,
I just might justify his fears about me.

SGANARELLE

(To Ariste:)
Well, teacher, there's what comes of what you teach.
Do you not shudder, hearing such a speech?

ARISTE

Brother, we should but smile at her discourse.
And yet her notions have a certain force:
All women like a bit of freedom, and
It's wrong to rule them with a heavy hand.
It isn't bolts and bars and strict controls
That give our wives and maidens virtuous souls;
No, honor keeps their feet on duty's path,
And not our harshness or our threatened wrath.
I say, indeed, that there's no woman known
Who's good and faithful through constraint alone.
We can't dictate a woman's every move:
If we're to sway her, it must be by love,
And I, whatever curbs I'd put upon her,
Would not feel safe were I to trust my honor
To one who was deterred from wronging me
Only by lack of opportunity.

SGANARELLE

What drivel!

ARISTE

As you like; but still I say
That we should school the young in a pleasant way,
And chide them very gently when they've erred,
Lest virtue come to seem a hateful word.
I've raised Léonor by maxims such as these;
I've not made crimes of little liberties;
To all her young desires I've given consent—
Of which, thank Heaven, I've no cause to repent.
I've let her see good company, and go
To balls, and plays, and every sort of show,
Such social pleasures being well designed,
I've always held, to form a youthful mind.
The world's a school in which we learn to live
By better lessons than any book could give.
She's fond of buying gowns, and bows and frills:
Well, what of that? I give her what she wills,
For gay attire's a thing we should permit
Young girls to enjoy, if we can pay for it.
She's pledged to wed me by her father's order,
But I shall not be overbearing toward her:
I well know that, in years, we're far apart,
And so I free her to consult her heart.
If the four thousand crowns I yearly earn,
My deep affection, and my dear concern
Can compensate, in her considered view,
For all the years which separate us two,
Then she shall wed me; if not, she'll choose another.
She might be happier without me, Brother,
And I had rather give her up than see
Her forced, against her will, to marry me.

SGANARELLE

How sweet he is! All sugar and spice! My, my!

ARISTE

Well, that's my nature, thank the Lord, and I
Deplore the too-strict training which has led
So many children to wish their parents dead.

SGANARELLE

The more one lets the young run wild, the greater
A task it is to discipline them later;
You'll view her willful habits with misgiving
When the time comes to change her mode of living.

ARISTE

Why should I change it?

SGANARELLE

Why?

ARISTE

Yes.

SGANARELLE

I don't know.

ARISTE

Is there any disgrace, do you think, in living so?

SGANARELLE

Oh come! If you marry her, will you still allow
The girlish freedoms you permit her now?

ARISTE

Why not?

SGANARELLE

Then you'll indulge her, I suppose,
In wearing ribbons, beauty spots and bows?

ARISTE

Of course.

SGANARELLE

And let her madly run about
To every ball, or fashionable rout?

ARISTE

Quite so.

SGANARELLE

You'll receive young gallants in your house?

ARISTE

Why, yes.

SGANARELLE

To make merry, and amuse your spouse?

ARISTE

Indeed.

SGANARELLE

And they'll pay her flowery compliments?

ARISTE

No doubt.

SGANARELLE

And you'll stand by at these events,
Looking entirely unconcerned and cool?

ARISTE

Most certainly.

SGANARELLE

Enough! You're an old fool.
(*To Isabelle:*)
Go in; you mustn't hear such shameful rot.

ARISTE

I'll trust my wife's fidelity, and shall not
Do otherwise, when married, than now I do.

SGANARELLE

How I'll enjoy it when she cuckolds you!

ARISTE

I don't know what the stars intend for me,
But if they should deny you cuckoldry
It won't be your fault, for you've taken great
Pains to deserve that horny-headed state.

SGANARELLE

Laugh on, my jester. It's wondrous to behold
A clown who's almost sixty winters old!

LÉONOR

If he should wed me, I'd never make him bear
The fate of which you speak; to that I'll swear.
But were I forced to wear your wedding ring,
I frankly couldn't promise anything.

LISETTE

We owe fidelity to them that trust us;
But cheating folk like you is simple justice.

23

SGANARELLE

Just hold your cursèd, ill-bred tongue, d'you hear?

ARISTE

You've brought this mockery on yourself, I fear.
Farewell. Do change your views, and realize
That locking up one's wife can be unwise.
Brother, your servant.

SGANARELLE

      I'm not *your* servant, Brother.
(Alone:)
Oh, but those three are made for one another!
What a fine household! An agèd maniac
With foppish clothing on his creaking back;
A girlish mistress who's a wild coquette;
Impudent servants; wisdom herself would get
Nothing but headaches by attempting to
Correct the ways of that unbalanced crew.
Lest Isabelle, in their loose company,
Should lose the sound ideas she's learned from me,
I'll send her back where she'll be safe from harm
Among the beans and turkeys of my farm.

Scene 3

Valère, Sganarelle, Ergaste.

VALÈRE

(At the rear of the stage.)
Ergaste, look: there's that Argus I abhor,
The guardian of the girl whom I adore.

SGANARELLE

(Thinking himself alone:)
It's altogether shocking, the decay
Of manners and of morals in our day!

VALÈRE

I'm going to accost him, if I can,
And strike up an acquaintance with the man.

SGANARELLE

(Thinking himself alone:)
Where are those standards, stern and absolute,
Which were the basis, once, of good repute?
Our wild young folk indulge their every whim,
And won't . . .

(Valère bows to Sganarelle, from a distance.)

VALÈRE

He didn't see me bow to him.

ERGASTE

Maybe he's blind on this side; what do you say
We walk around him?

SGANARELLE

(Thinking himself alone:)
                    I must end my stay.
Life in this city only serves to rouse
My worst . . .

VALÈRE

(Approaching bit by bit.)
    I *must* gain entrance to his house.

SGANARELLE

(Hearing a noise:)
Did I hear a voice?
(Thinking himself alone:)
      In the country, praise the Lord,
The follies of these times can be ignored.

ERGASTE

(To Valère:)
Go up to him.

SGANARELLE

(Once more hearing a noise:)
    Eh?
(Hearing no further sound:)
      My ears are ringing, I guess.
(Thinking himself alone:)
There, girls have simple pleasures, simple dress . . .
(He sees Valère bowing to him.)
What's this?

ERGASTE

(To Valère:)
  Get closer.

SGANARELLE

(Still staring at Valère:)
     There, no fops are seen . . .
(Valère bows to him again.)
What the devil—
(He turns and sees Ergaste bowing on the other side.)
    Another? Such bowing! What does it mean?

VALÈRE

Do I disrupt your thoughts, sir, by this greeting?

SGANARELLE

Perhaps.

VALÈRE

Forgive me; but this happy meeting
Is such a privilege, such a pleasure, too,
I couldn't forgo this chance to speak with you.

SGANARELLE

I see.

VALÈRE

And to assure you that I stand
Entirely at your service, heart and hand.

SGANARELLE

I'm sure of it.

VALÈRE

It's my happiness to be
Your neighbor, for which I thank my destiny.

SGANARELLE

Well put.

VALÈRE

But now, sir, have your heard the new
Gossip at court? Some think it may be true.

SGANARELLE

Does that concern me?

VALÈRE

No; but in such a matter
Folk sometimes like to hear the latest chatter.
Shall you go see the lavish preparations
For our new Dauphin's natal celebrations?

SGANARELLE

If I like.

VALÈRE

Ah, Paris affords us, you must own,
A hundred pleasures which elsewhere are unknown;
The country offers nothing that compares.
What are your pastimes?

SGANARELLE

Tending to my affairs.

VALÈRE

Still, one needs relaxation, and the brain,
From too much serious use, can suffer strain.
What do you do 'twixt supper time and bed?

SGANARELLE

Just what I please.

VALÈRE

Ah, sir, that's nicely said;
A wise reply; we all should see life thus,
And only do what truly pleases us.
Some evening, if you're free of business, I'll
Drop by, if I may, and chat with you a while.

SGANARELLE

Your servant.

Scene 4

Valère, Ergaste.

VALÈRE

That crackpot! What did you make of him?

ERGASTE

He gives gruff answers, and his manner's grim.

VALÈRE

Oh, I can't bear it!

ERGASTE

What?

VALÈRE

It irks my soul
That the one I love is under the control
Of a fierce, sharp-eyed dragon who will never
Allow her any liberty whatever.

ERGASTE

Why, that's to your advantage; the situation
Should fill your heart with hope and expectation.
Cheer up; you have no cause to feel undone.
A woman closely watched is halfway won,
And a harsh husband or a crabbed sire
Is just what any lover should desire.
I don't chase women; for that I have no talent;

29

And I do not profess to be a gallant;
But I've served woman-chasers by the score
Who told me often that nothing pleased them more
Than meeting with those fractious husbands who
Come grumbling home and scold all evening through,
Those brutes who groundlessly mistrust their wives,
Checking on every moment of their lives,
And act proprietary and unpleasant
When young admirers of their wives are present.
"All this," they said, "is favorable to us.
The lady's pique at being treated thus,
And the warm sympathy which we then express,
Can pave the way to amorous success."
In short, if you have hopes of Isabelle,
Her guardian's cranky ways may serve you well.

VALÈRE

But for four months I've been her worshipper,
And never had one chance to speak with her!

ERGASTE

Love makes men clever; but it's not done much for you.
In your place, I'd—

VALÈRE

But what was there to do?
She's never seen without that beast nearby;
There are no servants in his house whom I
Could tempt with little gifts, and thus obtain
As helpers in my amorous campaign.

ERGASTE

Then she doesn't know, as yet, of your devotion?

VALÈRE

Well, as to that I have no certain notion.
Whenever that barbarian's taken her out,
She's seen me, for I've shadowed her about
And sought by fervent glances to impart
The raging passion that is in my heart.
My eyes have spoken boldly; but how well
She's understood their language, who can tell?

ERGASTE

Such language can be hard to fathom, when
It's not interpreted by tongue or pen.

VALÈRE

How can I end this anguishing ordeal,
And learn if she's aware of what I feel?
Think of some stratagem.

ERGASTE

That's what we must discover.
Let's go inside a while, and think it over.

Act Two

Scene 1

Isabelle, Sganarelle.

SGANARELLE

That's quite enough; I know the house, and can,
From what you tell me, recognize the man.

ISABELLE

(*Aside:*)
O Heaven! be gracious now, and lend your aid
To the artful plot my innocent love has laid.

SGANARELLE

You've learned, I gather, that his name's Valère?

ISABELLE

Yes.

SGANARELLE

Go then; don't fret; I'll handle this affair.
I'll speak at once to that young lunatic.

ISABELLE

(As she goes in:)
It's bold for a girl to play this sort of trick;
But since I'm harshly and unjustly used,
I hope, by all fair minds, to be excused.

Scene 2

Sganarelle, Ergaste, Valère.

SGANARELLE

(At Valère's door.)
Well here's the house. I'll act without delay.
Who goes there? Ah, I'm dreaming . . . Hullo, I say!
It doesn't surprise me, knowing what now I know,
That he paid court to me an hour ago;
But I'll soon dash the hopes of this fond lover—
(To Ergaste, who has come out in haste:)
You clumsy oaf! Do you mean to knock me over?
Why stand there like a post and block the door?

VALÈRE

I regret, sir—

SGANARELLE

Ah! It's you I'm looking for.

VALÈRE

I, sir?

SGANARELLE

Yes, you. Your name's Valère, I find.

VALÈRE

It is.

SGANARELLE

A word with you, if you don't mind.

VALÈRE

May I serve you somehow? I should be proud to do—

SGANARELLE

No, but there's something I can do for you,
And that is why I've sought your house, and found you.

VALÈRE

You've come to my house, sir!

SGANARELLE

Yes. Need that astound you?

VALÈRE

It does indeed, and I'm in ecstasies
At this great honor—

SGANARELLE

Forget the honor, please.

VALÈRE

Won't you come in?

SGANARELLE

I see no need of that.

35

VALÈRE

I beg you, sir.

SGANARELLE

I'll stay where I am; that's flat.

VALÈRE

I'd hear you better if we went within.

SGANARELLE

I shall not budge.

VALÈRE

Ah well, I must give in.
(To Ergaste:)
Our guest won't enter, but he must have a seat.
Quick, bring a chair.

SGANARELLE

I'll talk to you on my feet.

VALÈRE

But how can I let you—

SGANARELLE

What infernal stalling!

VALÈRE

Such incivility would be appalling.

SGANARELLE

What in the world is more uncivil, pray,
Than not to hear what people want to say?

VALÈRE

I'll do as you wish, then.

SGANARELLE

That's a splendid notion.
(They go to great lengths of ceremony, in putting on their hats.)
These courtesies are a waste of time and motion.
Now, will you listen?

VALÈRE

I shall, sir, with delight.

SGANARELLE

Do you know that I'm the guardian of a quite
Young girl, who's rather pretty; that we dwell
Nearby, and that her name is Isabelle?

VALÈRE

Yes.

SGANARELLE

I won't say, then, what you know already.
Do you know, likewise, that her charms have led me
To feelings other than a guardian's pride,
And that her destiny is to be my bride?

VALÈRE

No.

SGANARELLE

Then I tell you so. And I bid you cease
Your warm advances, and leave the girl in peace.

VALÈRE

I, sir?

37

SGANARELLE

You. Don't deny that you pursue her.

VALÈRE

Who told you, then, of my devotion to her?

SGANARELLE

People whose testimony one can credit.

VALÈRE

But who?

SGANARELLE

She herself.

VALÈRE

She?

SGANARELLE

She. That's twice I've said it.
That good young woman, who, since she was small,
Has loved me, came just now and told me all,
And charged me, furthermore, to let you know
That when, of late, you've dogged her footsteps so,
Her heart, which your attentions scandalize,
Read all too well the language of your eyes;
That what you feel for her is all too clear,
And that 'twill be no use to persevere
In shows of passion which can only be
Offensive to a heart that's pledged to me.

VALÈRE

You say that she, of her own accord, besought you—

SGANARELLE

Yes, to convey the message that I've brought you.
She adds that, having plumbed your heart, she would
Have made herself much sooner understood,
If she'd been able, through some messenger,
To express the feelings which arose in her;
At last, in her extreme frustration, she
Had no recourse but to make use of me,
In order to inform you, as I've said,
That I'm the man she loves and means to wed,
That the sheep's eyes you've made were made in vain,
And that, if you have any sort of brain,
You'll take your passion elsewhere. For now, farewell.
I've told you everything I had to tell.

VALÈRE

Good heavens, Ergaste, what do you make of this?

SGANARELLE

(Sotto voce, moving away:)
How stunned he looks!

ERGASTE

(Sotto voce, to Valère:)
                    It's my analysis
That you need not be troubled for a minute.
This message has a secret meaning in it,
And wasn't sent by someone who desires
To terminate the love which she inspires.

SGANARELLE

(Aside:)
He takes it well.

VALÈRE

(Sotto voce, to Ergaste:)
     You think her words implied—?

ERGASTE

(Sotto voce:)
Yes . . . But he's watching us; let's go inside.

SGANARELLE

(Alone:)
My, what confusion's written in his visage!
Clearly, he didn't expect so harsh a message.
Let me call Isabelle. In her we find
The effect of sound instruction on the mind.
So perfect is her virtue that if a man
Dares look at her, she puts him under ban.

Scene 3

Isabelle, Sganarelle.

ISABELLE

(Sotto voce, as she enters:)
I fear that, in his passion, my lover may
Not fathom what my message meant to say;
And so I must, since I'm a captive here,
Risk yet another to make my meaning clear.

SGANARELLE

Well, I am back.

ISABELLE

     What happened?

SGANARELLE

Your words quite dashed
Your lover's spirits; he's utterly abashed.
He sought to deny his passion, but once he knew
That you had sent me, and that I spoke for you,
The fellow stood there speechless and nonplussed.
He won't be troubling us again, I trust.

ISABELLE

Ah, won't he, though! I greatly fear he will,
And that he'll give us much more trouble still.

SGANARELLE

What grounds do you have for such a premonition?

ISABELLE

You'd hardly left the house upon your mission
When I went to the window for a breath of air
And saw a young man on that corner there,
Who, much to my amazement, shortly came
And greeted me in my admirer's name,
And then, with further impudence, tossed into
My room a box which held a billet-doux.
I would have thrown it back to him, but his feet
Had far too quickly borne him up the street,
Leaving me full of outrage and distress.

SGANARELLE

Just think of it! Such guile, such craftiness!

ISABELLE

Duty requires that I send back again
Both box and letter to this cursèd swain,
But who's to run the errand I cannot say.
I dare not ask you—

SGANARELLE

My sweet, of course you may.
You prove your love of me by what you ask,
And I accept with joy this little task:
I can't express my pleasure.

ISABELLE

Then take this, do.

SGANARELLE

Let's see, now, what he's dared to say to you.

ISABELLE

Oh, heavens! Don't break the seal.

SGANARELLE

Not open it? Why?

ISABELLE

He'd think 'twas I it had been opened by.
A decent girl should never read the tender
Communications which young men may send her:
To show such curiosity betrays
A secret appetite for flattering praise.
I think it right, then, that this missive be
Returned unopened, and most speedily,
So that Valère will learn this very day
How much I scorn him, and will without delay
Discard the hopes which he's invested in me,
And make no more absurd attempts to win me.

SGANARELLE

Her point's well taken; this young girl reasons rightly.
My dear, your virtue and good sense delight me:

My teachings have borne fruit, I see with pride,
And you are worthy indeed to be my bride.

ISABELLE

Still, I won't oppose your wishes; I wouldn't dare to.
You have the letter; open it, if you care to.

SGANARELLE

No, no, your reasons cannot be contested.
I'll go and do this errand you've requested,
Make a brief call nearby—ten minutes at best—
And then return to set your mind at rest.

Scene 4

Sganarelle, Ergaste.

SGANARELLE

(Alone:)
It floods my soul with rapture to have found
This girl so utterly discreet and sound!
I have in my house a pearl of purest honor!
She treats a love-glance as a slur upon her!
A billet-doux does nothing but offend her!
By *my* hand, she returns it to the sender!
I wonder if my brother's ward, in such
A situation, would have done as much.
This proves, by Heaven, that girls are what we make them.
Ho, there!

(He knocks on Valère's door.)

ERGASTE

Yes?

SGANARELLE

These are your master's property; take them.
Tell him that no more letters need be sent
In small gold boxes; it's most impertinent,
And he has greatly angered Isabelle.
See, it's not even been opened: He can tell
By that how low is her regard for him,
And that the prospects for his love are dim.

Scene 5

Valère, Ergaste.

VALÈRE

What were you given by that surly brute?

ERGASTE

A letter, sir, and a gold box to boot.
He claims that you sent Isabelle this letter,
Which, he declares, has mightily upset her.
She's sent it back unopened. Come, read it, sir.
Let's see how accurate my conjectures were.

VALÈRE

(Reading:)

"This letter will doubtless surprise you, and both in my
decision to write it, and in the manner of its delivery, I must
seem very rash indeed; but I find myself in such a situation that
I cannot observe the proprieties any longer. My just aversion to
a marriage with which I am threatened in six days' time, has
made me ready to dare anything; and in my determination to
escape that bondage by whatever means, I have thought it better to turn to you than to embrace Despair. Still, you must not

think that you owe everything to my afflicted state; it is not the predicament in which I find myself that has given rise to my feelings for you; but it hastens my avowal of them, and causes me to overstep the bounds of decorum prescribed for my sex. Whether I am soon to be yours is now entirely up to you; I wait only for a declaration of your heart's intentions before acquainting you with the resolution I have taken; but do be aware that time is pressing, and that two hearts attuned by love should need but few words to come to an understanding."

ERGASTE

Well, sir! Was this a clever ruse, or not?
For a young girl, she lays a brilliant plot!
Love is a game, it seems, that she can play.

VALÈRE

Oh, she's adorable in every way!
This evidence of her wit and warmth of heart
Doubles my love for her, which had its start
When first her beauty caused my head to swim . . .

ERGASTE

Here comes our dupe; think what you'll say to him.

Scene 6

Sganarelle, Valère, Ergaste.

SGANARELLE

(Thinking himself alone:)
Ah, thrice and four times may the heavens bless
This law which bans extravagance in dress!
No more will husbands' troubles be so great,

And women's frivolous cravings will abate.
Oh, how I thank the king for such decrees,
And how I wish that, for men's further ease
Of mind, he'd ban not only lace and frills
But coquetry and its attendant ills!
I've bought this edict so that Isabelle
May read it aloud to me, and learn it well.
Some evening, when her tasks are all complete,
We'll have it for an after-supper treat.
(*Perceiving Valère:*)
Well, do you plan now, Mister Goldilocks,
To send more love notes in that gilded box?
You thought you'd found a young coquette who'd be
Fond of intrigue and honeyed flattery,
But what a chill response your offerings got!
Believe me, lad, you waste your powder and shot
She's a sensible girl; it's me she loves; why aim
At one who scorns you? Go hunt for easier game.

                    VALÈRE
Indeed, your merits, which all the world admires,
Are a hopeless barrier, sir, to my desires.
Much as I love her, it's folly on my part
To vie with you for Isabelle's hand and heart.

                  SGANARELLE
Quite right, it's folly.

                    VALÈRE
            I wouldn't, furthermore,
Have yielded to the charms which I adore,
Had I foreseen that I was doomed to meet,
In you, a rival no man could defeat.

46

SGANARELLE

I quite believe you.

VALÈRE

I now can hope no longer,
And freely grant, sir, that your claim's the stronger.

SGANARELLE

Well done.

VALÈRE

In this, I merely do what's right,
For, sir, your many virtues shine so bright
That I'd do wrong to take a grudging view
Of Isabelle's great tenderness toward you.

SGANARELLE

Of course.

VALÈRE

Your victory, then, I don't contest.
But, sir, I pray you (it's the sole request
Of a poor lover whom you have overthrown,
And whose great pains are due to you alone),
I pray you, sir, to say to Isabelle
That in these months I've spent beneath her spell
My love's been pure, and never entertained
A thought by which her honor might be pained.

SGANARELLE

Agreed.

VALÈRE

That the one thing I desired of life
Was that I might obtain her for my wife,

47

Till fate obstructed my desire, revealing
That she was bound to you by tenderest feeling.

SGANARELLE

Good. Good.

VALÈRE

That, whatever happens, she must not
Think that her charms will ever be forgot;
That, let the heavens treat me as they may,
My fate's to love her till my dying day;
And that your merits, of which I stand in awe,
Are the sole reason why I now withdraw.

SGANARELLE

Well said; I'll go at once and give her this
Message, which she will scarcely take amiss.
But if I may advise you, do your best
To drive this fruitless passion from your breast.
Farewell.

ERGASTE

(To Valère:)
What a perfect dupe!

SGANARELLE

(Alone:)
It makes me sad
To see the anguish of this lovesick lad;
'Twas his misfortune to suppose that he
Could storm a fortress long since won by me.

48

Scene 7

Sganarelle, Isabelle.

SGANARELLE

Never did any swain so hang his head
To see his billet-doux come back unread.
He's lost all hope, and will no longer woo you,
But begs me to convey this message to you:
That in his passion, he never entertained
A thought by which your honor might be pained,
And that the one thing he desired of life
Was that he might obtain you for his wife,
Till fate obstructed his desire, revealing
That you were bound to me by tenderest feeling;
That, whatsoever happens, you must not
Think that your charms will ever be forgot;
That, let the heavens treat him as they may,
His fate's to love you till his dying day;
And that my merits, of which he stands in awe,
Are the sole cause which leads him to withdraw.
Those are his touching words; I cannot hate him;
He's a decent fellow, and I commiserate him.

ISABELLE

(*Aside:*)
Those sweet words but confirm my heart's surmise;
I read his pure intentions in his eyes.

SGANARELLE

Eh? What did you say?

ISABELLE

I said that I'm distressed
To hear you pity a man I so detest,

49

And that, if you truly loved me, you would share
My rage at the affronts he's made me bear.

SGANARELLE

But he didn't know, dear, that your heart was mine;
And his intentions were so pure and fine
That one can hardly—

ISABELLE

　　　　　Is it well-intended, pray,
To seize a person, and carry her away?
Would a man of honor think it a noble course
To snatch me from you, and marry me by force?
As if I were the kind of girl who could
Survive such insults to her maidenhood!

SGANARELLE

Do you mean to tell me—

ISABELLE

　　　　　Yes; this brutish lover
Talks of abducting me, I now discover.
I don't know by what secret means he can
Have learned so very quickly of your plan
To marry me within a week or so,
Since only yesterday you let me know;
But he intends to strike at once, I find,
Before our loves and fates can be combined.

SGANARELLE

Well, this is bad indeed.

ISABELLE

　　　　　Oh, no! I'm sure
He's a decent fellow, whose aims are fine and pure!

SGANARELLE

This is no joke; he's wrong in the extreme.

ISABELLE

Your mildness prompts him to this madcap scheme.
If you'd been harsh with him just now, he would
Have feared your wrath and mine, and stopped for good;
But even after his letter was returned
He hatched the shocking plot of which I've learned,
Convinced in spite of all, it would appear,
That in my heart of hearts I hold him dear,
That I am loath to wed you, and cannot wait
For him to free me from my captive state.

SGANARELLE

He's mad.

ISABELLE

With you, he knows how to disguise
His feelings, and pull the wool over your eyes.
But his fair words make sport of you, believe me.
It does, I'm forced to tell you, deeply grieve me
That after all I've done, for honor's sake,
To balk the vile advances of this rake,
I still must find myself exposed to these
Shameful designs and base conspiracies!

SGANARELLE

There, there; don't worry.

ISABELLE

I swear, if you do not
Rebuke him fiercely for this impudent plot,

And find a way to put a stop at once
To this bold rogue's continual affronts,
I shall embrace some desperate solution
And, once for all, escape his persecution.

SGANARELLE

Come, come, my little dear, don't fret and frown;
I'll go at once and give him a dressing-down.

ISABELLE

Tell him it's useless to play innocent,
That I've been fully informed of his intent,
And that, whatever he may now devise,
I challenge him to take me by surprise;
Tell him he wastes his time, and urge him to
Remember what my feelings are toward you;
And add that, lest he pay a bitter price,
He'd best not wait for me to warn him twice.

SGANARELLE

I'll say what's needful.

ISABELLE

Show him I mean all this
By speaking it with gravest emphasis.

SGANARELLE

Yes, yes, I'll say it all, and I'll be stern.

ISABELLE

I'll wait impatiently for your return.
Please hasten back to me with all your might:
I'm desolate when you are out of sight.

SGANARELLE

Fear not, I'll soon be back with you, my sweet.
(*Alone:*)
Was ever a girl more prudent, more discreet?
How happy I am! How fortunate to find
A wife so suited to my heart and mind!
Yes, that is how our women ought to be—
Not like some wives I know, whose coquetry
And bold amours have managed to embarrass
Their wretched mates before the whole of Paris.
(*Knocking at Valère's door:*)
Ho there, my fine and enterprising swain!

Scene 8

Valère, Sganarelle, Ergaste.

VALÈRE

What brings you back, sir?

SGANARELLE

Your follies, once again.

VALÈRE

What?

SGANARELLE

Come, you understand my reference.
Frankly, I thought that you had better sense.
You've hoaxed me with fine speeches, and continue
To harbor vain and foolish hopes within you.

I've wished to treat you gently, but—see here—
If this goes on, my rage will be severe.
Aren't you ashamed that you, a gentleman,
Should stoop to such skullduggery, should plan
To abduct a decent girl, and cheat her of
A marriage which would bring her joy and love?

VALÈRE

Sir, where did you hear this curious news? Do tell.

SGANARELLE

Let's not dissemble: My source is Isabelle,
Who for the last time tells you, through my voice,
That she's informed you plainly of her choice;
That she's mine, and hates this plot that you've devised;
That she'd rather die than be thus compromised,
And that there will be dire results, unless
You put an end to all this foolishness.

VALÈRE

If that is truly what she said, it seems
That there's no future for my ardent dreams:
Those plain words tell me I must yield at last
And bow before the sentence she has passed.

SGANARELLE

If? Do you doubt, then, that they came from her,
These words I've brought you as her messenger?
Would you care to hear them from her lips? I'm quite
Prepared to allow it, just to set you right.
Follow me, then, and learn from her directly
Whom she prefers, and if I spoke correctly.

Scene 9

Isabelle, Sganarelle, Valère.

ISABELLE

You've brought him here—to me? With what design?
Have you taken *his* side, and forsaken mine?
Have his merits charmed you so that I'm to be
Compelled to love him, and bear his company?

SGANARELLE

Ah, no. I'd never give you up, my precious.
But he thinks that my reports were meretricious,
That I falsified your feelings when I stated
That you were fond of me, and he was hated;
Therefore I'd have you speak to him, and dispose
Of this delusion on which his hopes repose.

ISABELLE

(To Valère:)
What! When I've bared my whole soul to your eyes,
Can you still doubt where my affection lies?

VALÈRE

Madam, this gentleman's reports were such,
I own, as to surprise me very much:
Frankly, I doubted them; and this last decree,
Which sentences my heart to misery,
So stuns me that I dare request of you
That you repeat those words, if they were true.

ISABELLE

No sentence that I've passed should have surprised you:
Of what I feel, my plain words have advised you,

But since my judgments had both truth and strength
I don't mind stating them at greater length.
Yes, hear me, gentlemen, and believe me, too:
Fate here presents two objects to my view
Who agitate my heart with sentiments
Quite different, though equally intense.
The first, whom honor bids me choose, I deem
Worthy of all my love, all my esteem;
The other one's affection gains from me
All my resentment and antipathy.
The presence of the first is dear and sweet,
And makes my soul's felicity complete;
As for the other, my heart is seized by grim
Hatred and horror at the sight of him.
The first I long to marry, while if I
Were forced to wed the other, I'd wish to die.
But I've now said enough of what I feel,
And borne too long the pains of this ordeal;
It's time for him I love to terminate
Decisively the hopes of him I hate,
And by a happy marriage deliver me
From torments worse than death itself could be.

SGANARELLE

There, there: I'll grant your wishes, little one.

ISABELLE

I'll have no happiness till that is done.

SGANARELLE

You'll soon be happy.

ISABELLE

It's scandalous, I know,
For a young girl to declare her passions so.

SGANARELLE

No, no.

ISABELLE

Yet in my present state of strain
I take the liberty of being plain,
And cannot blush for the fervent things I've said
Of one to whom I feel already wed.

SGANARELLE

Of course not, sweetest angel, dearest dear.

ISABELLE

Let him now prove his love at last.

SGANARELLE

Yes—here—
Come kiss my hand.

ISABELLE

Let him delay no more,
But speed the nuptial day I'm yearning for,
And take my promise now that none but he
Shall ever speak his marriage vows to me.

(She pretends to embrace Sganarelle, and gives Valère her hand to kiss.)

SGANARELLE

Haha, my pretty duck, my pussycat!
You shall not pine for long, I promise that:
There, now! *(To Valère)* You see, she cares for me alone.
I didn't prompt her; those words were all her own.

VALÈRE

Well, madam, you've made your feelings clear indeed:
I grasp your wishes, and shall pay them heed.
I'll rid you very soon, you may be sure,
Of him whose presence you can not endure.

ISABELLE

Do so, and I'll be infinitely grateful;
For merely to behold him is so hateful,
So insupportable, so odious—

SGANARELLE

Now, now.

ISABELLE

I offend you, then, by speaking thus?

SGANARELLE

Oh, mercy, not in the least. But I confess
I feel some pity for the man's distress;
You put your adverse feelings too severely.

ISABELLE

At a time like this, they can't be put too clearly.

VALÈRE

Well, I'll oblige you. In three days from this date
You'll see no more the object of your hate.

ISABELLE

Thank Heaven. Farewell.

SGANARELLE

(To Valère:)
        I'm sorry for your pain,
But—

VALÈRE

No, you'll not hear me whimper or complain:
In judging us, M*adame's* been most judicious,
And I'll now strive to gratify her wishes.
Farewell.

SGANARELLE

      Poor lad, he's utterly undone.
Come, I'm her other self; embrace me, son.

(He embraces Valère.)

Scene 10

Isabelle, Sganarelle.

SGANARELLE

He's much to be pitied.

ISABELLE

I feel no such emotion.

SGANARELLE

In any case, I'm touched by your devotion,
My sweet, and it deserves some recompense:
A week's too long to keep you in suspense;
Tomorrow, then, shall be our wedding day.

ISABELLE

Tomorrow?

SGANARELLE

From modesty, you feign dismay,
But I well know what joy my words created,
And that you wish we were already mated.

ISABELLE

But—

SGANARELLE

Let's prepare for the wedding; come, be quick.

ISABELLE

(Aside:)
Inspire me, Heaven! I need another trick.

Act Three

Scene 1

Isabelle.

ISABELLE

(*Alone:*)
Yes, death is far less dire to contemplate
Than a forced marriage to an unloved mate,
And I should not be censured, but forgiven
For any subterfuge to which I'm driven.
Time passes; night has fallen; I now must dare
To trust my fate and fortune to Valère.

Scene 2

Sganarelle, Isabelle.

SGANARELLE

(*Enters, muttering to himself:*)
That's done. Tomorrow, when the magistrate—

ISABELLE

Oh, Heaven!

SGANARELLE

Is it you, dear? Where are you going so late?
You told me, when I left, that you desired
To go to your chamber, being a little tired;
You even begged that I, upon returning,
Would not disturb you till tomorrow morning.

ISABELLE

That's true, but—

SGANARELLE

Yes?

ISABELLE

You see my hesitation;
I fear that you won't like the explanation.

SGANARELLE

Come, tell me.

ISABELLE

You'll be amazed. The reason for
My going out is sister Léonor;
She's borrowed my chamber, which she means to use
As part of a disreputable ruse.

SGANARELLE

What?

ISABELLE

Would you believe it? She loves that rogue whom we
Have just sent packing.

SGANARELLE

Valère?

ISABELLE

Yes, desperately:
I've never seen an ardor so intense;
And you may judge her passion's violence
By her coming here, at such an hour, alone,
To make the anguish of her spirit known.
She told me that she surely will expire
Unless she can obtain her heart's desire,
That for a year and more, Valère and she
Were fervent lovers, meeting secretly,
And that, when first they loved, they traded vows,
Each promising to become the other's spouse.

SGANARELLE

The wretched girl!

ISABELLE

That, knowing how I'd sent
The man she worships into banishment,
She begged me to allow her, since her heart
Would break if he were ever to depart,
To bid him in my name to come tonight
And stand beneath my window, so that she might
Impersonate my voice, and in a vein
Of sweet indulgence move him to remain—
Thus using for her own ends, as you see,
The warm regard she knows he feels for me.

SGANARELLE

And do you condone—

ISABELLE

I? No, I'm much put out.
"Sister," I said, "you're mad beyond a doubt.
Do you not blush to throw your heart away
On a fickle sort who changes every day,
And shame your sex by choosing him instead
Of the trusting man whom Heaven would have you wed?"

SGANARELLE

Just what the fool deserves; I'm most content.

ISABELLE

In short, with many a furious argument
I chided her behavior, and said I quite
Refused to let her use my room tonight;
But she poured such entreaties in my ears,
And heaved such sighs, and wept so many tears,
And said so often that she would despair
Unless I granted her impassioned prayer,
That love for her compelled me to accede.
Then, to secure the witness I might need
To clear my name, I thought to ask my friend
Lucrèce, whose many virtues you commend,
To spend the night with me. But ere I could go,
Your quick return surprised me, as you know.

SGANARELLE

No! All this jugglery I won't permit.
To spite my brother, I might agree to it;
But from the street they might be seen and heard;
And she on whom my hand's to be conferred
Must be not only chaste by disposition,
And gently bred, but quite above suspicion.
Let's send this wanton girl away, and teach her—

64

ISABELLE

Oh, no; you'd be too harsh with the poor creature;
And she might very justly take offense
At my betrayal of her confidence.
Since you require me to refuse my sister,
Stay here, at least, until I have dismissed her.

SGANARELLE

Well, do so, then.

ISABELLE

Pray find some place of hiding,
And let her leave without reproach or chiding.

SGANARELLE

For love of you I'll curb my anger, dear;
But just as soon as she is out of here
I'll run and find my brother; 'twill be a rare
Pleasure to let him know of this affair.

ISABELLE

In your account, please leave my name unsaid.
Good night: When she has left, I'll go to bed.

SGANARELLE

Until tomorrow, my pet. I cannot wait
To see my brother, and tell him of his fate!
He's proven a fool, for all his glib conceit:
Not for a million would I miss this treat.

ISABELLE

(Inside the house.)
Yes, Sister, I'm sorry that you're so distressed,
But I can't grant the favor you request:

The danger to my honor would be too great.
Farewell. Best hurry home; it's growing late.

SGANARELLE

She'll leave, I wager, feeling cross and sore.
For fear she may come back, I'll lock the door.

ISABELLE

(Aside, as she emerges in disguise:)
Help my cause, Heaven; don't abandon me.

SGANARELLE

(Aside:)
Where is she going? I'll follow a bit, and see.

ISABELLE

(Aside:)
At any rate, this dark night serves my end.

SGANARELLE

(Aside:)
She's gone to Valère's house! What can she intend?

Scene 3

Valère, Isabelle, Sganarelle.

VALÈRE

(Coming out in haste.)
Yes, yes; tonight, if some way can be found
To tell her . . . Who's there?

ISABELLE

Valère, don't make a sound.
You needn't go out; I'm here; it's Isabelle.

SGANARELLE

(*Aside:*)
No, you're not she; what a brazen lie you tell!
She lives by honor, whereas you flirt with shame,
And falsely have assumed her voice and name.

ISABELLE

(*To Valère:*)
However, unless your goal is matrimony—

VALÈRE

My heart is moved by that sweet purpose only.
Tomorrow, I assure you, I shall seize
The chance to wed you in any church you please.

SGANARELLE

(*Aside:*)
Poor hoodwinked fool!

VALÈRE

Come in, and have no fear;
That dupe, your guardian, cannot touch you here,
And ere I let him sunder me from you
This arm of mine will run him through and through.

SGANARELLE

(*Alone:*)
Oh, rest assured that I won't deprive you of
This shameless girl, who's so enslaved by love;
That what you've promised her does not aggrieve me,

67

And that I'll *make* you marry her, believe me!
Yes, he must be surprised with that young doxy:
Both as her well-respected father's proxy
And for her sister's name, I must see to it
That she avoids disgrace, if I can do it.
Ho, there!

(He knocks at the door of a Magistrate.)

Scene 4

Sganarelle, a Magistrate, a Notary, an Attendant with a lantern.

MAGISTRATE

Yes?

SGANARELLE

Magistrate, I'm glad you're here.
You're needed, sir, in your official gear.
Please follow me, and bring that lantern, too.

MAGISTRATE

We were going—

SGANARELLE

But this is urgent.

MAGISTRATE

What must I do?

SGANARELLE

Go in there, and take two culprits by surprise
Who should be joined by lawful marriage ties.

I know the girl: She, trusting in the vows
Of one Valère, was lured into his house.
She comes of good and noble family, yet—

MAGISTRATE

If that's your purpose, we're indeed well met,
For we have a notary with us.

SGANARELLE

That would be you, sir?

NOTARY

Yes; a king's notary.

MAGISTRATE

A man of honor too, sir.

SGANARELLE

Of course. Well, use that door—tread softly, eh?—
And don't let anybody get away.
You shall be well rewarded for this endeavor;
Don't let them try to grease your palm, however.

MAGISTRATE

What! Do you think that a jurist of my station—?

SGANARELLE

I meant no slur upon your occupation.
I'll go at once and fetch my brother. Kindly
Allow your lantern-bearer to walk behind me.
(*Aside:*)
Now, gentle Brother, I'll pay you a cheery visit.
Hello!

(*He knocks at Ariste's door.*)

Scene 5

Ariste, Sganarelle.

ARISTE

Who's knocking? Ah there, Brother! What is it?

SGANARELLE

Come, my wise pedagogue, my agèd beau,
There are pretty doings of which you ought to know.

ARISTE

How's that?

SGANARELLE

I bring you pleasant tidings.

ARISTE

Well?

SGANARELLE

Where is your Léonor tonight, pray tell?

ARISTE

Why do you ask? As I recall, she's gone
To a friend's house, for a ball.

SGANARELLE

Ha! Well, come on
And see what sort of ball such girls prefer.

ARISTE

What are you saying?

SGANARELLE

How well you've tutored her!
"It does no good to censure and upbraid;
No, it's by kindness that young minds are swayed;
It isn't bolts and bars and strict controls
That give our wives and maidens virtuous souls;
Too much constraint can make them misbehave,
And a bit of freedom's what all women crave."
Well, she's been free in the extreme, I'd say,
And her virtue grows more easy every day.

ARISTE

What are you getting at? I cannot quite—

SGANARELLE

Ah, dearest elder Brother, this serves you right!
I wouldn't miss it; you shall now find out
What your crazed theories have brought about.
See how these girls reflect what they've been taught;
Mine flees from gallants, yours chooses to be caught.

ARISTE

If you won't stop riddling—

SGANARELLE

The riddle of this affair
Is that her ball's at the house of young Valère;
That I saw her steal by night into his place,
And that she's, even now, in his embrace.

ARISTE

Who?

SGANARELLE

Léonor.

71

ARISTE

Please, please, let's have no jokes.

SGANARELLE

He dares dismiss my story as a hoax!
Poor fellow, I've told you—and I say once more—
That at Valère's you'll find your Léonor.
Know, too, that they were pledged to marry, well
Before he dreamt of courting Isabelle.

ARISTE

This tale's preposterous. You cannot mean it.

SGANARELLE

He won't believe it, even when he's seen it!
This drives me mad. Old age without a brain
(Tapping his forehead:)
Is not worth much.

ARISTE

Come, Brother, do you maintain—

SGANARELLE

Lord, no! I maintain nothing. Just follow me,
And you'll be freed from all uncertainty.
You'll see if I lie, and if it isn't so
That their troths were plighted more than a year ago.

ARISTE

Does it seem likely that she would embark
On such a course, and leave *me* in the dark,
When, all her life, I've looked with an entire
Indulgence on her every young desire,

And promised always that I'd not prevent
Her heart from freely following its bent?

SGANARELLE

Come, let your own eyes judge how matters stand.
A magistrate and notary are on hand:
The promised marriage should at once take place,
I think, to rescue her from more disgrace.
You, I assume, care something for your honor,
And would not wed her with this stain upon her—
Unless you fancy that your liberal vision
And fine ideas could save you from derision.

ARISTE

To claim another's heart against her will
Is something I would scorn to do. But still
I'm not convinced that—

SGANARELLE

How you do run on!
Let's go, or we'll be chattering here till dawn.

Scene 6

Sganarelle, Ariste, the Magistrate, the Notary.

MAGISTRATE

There's no need for compulsion, gentlemen;
If all you want is to see them married, then
I here and now can give you peace of mind.
Both parties, I am told, are so inclined,
And here is a signed statement from Valère
That he means to wed the girl now in his care.

73

ARISTE

And the girl's—?

MAGISTRATE

Locked in, and won't come out unless
You grant their wish for wedded happiness.

Scene 7

Valère, the Magistrate, the Notary, Sganarelle, Ariste.

VALÈRE

(At the window of his house.)
No, gentlemen; none shall enter here till you've
Assured me formally that you approve.
You know me, sirs; I've done what I must do
And signed the instrument they'll show to you.
If you are willing, then, for us to marry,
Your signatures are all that's necessary;
If not, you'll have to take my life before
You rob me of the one whom I adore.

SGANARELLE

No, we'll not rob you; set your mind at rest.
(Sotto voce, aside:)
He still believes that Isabelle is his guest:
Well, let him think it.

ARISTE

(To Valère:)
But is it Léonor—?

SGANARELLE

(To Ariste:)
Be quiet.

ARISTE

But—

SGANARELLE

Hush.

ARISTE

I want to know—

SGANARELLE

Once more,
Will you be quiet?

VALÈRE

In any case, good sirs,
Isabelle has my pledge, as I have hers.
Do think it over: I'm not so poor a catch
That you should make objection to the match.

ARISTE

(To Sganarelle:)
The name he said was—

SGANARELLE

Quiet! When this is through,
You shall know everything. *(To Valère)* Yes, without more ado,
We both agree that you shall be the spouse
Of her who is at present in your house.

MAGISTRATE

Just how this contract puts it, to the letter.
The name's left blank, because we've not yet met her.
Sign here. The girl can do so by and by.

VALÈRE

I agree to that.

SGANARELLE

With my whole heart, so do I.
(Aside:)
What a laugh I soon shall have! *(To Ariste)* Sign, Brother dear;
You should go first.

ARISTE

All this is so unclear—

SGANARELLE

Sign, sign, you idiot! What are you waiting for?

ARISTE

He speaks of Isabelle, you of Léonor.

SGANARELLE

What if it's she? Are you not willing, Brother,
To let these two keep faith with one another?

ARISTE

Surely.

SGANARELLE

Then sign, and I shall do the same.

ARISTE

Very well; but I'm baffled.

SGANARELLE
I'll soon explain the game.

MAGISTRATE
We shall return, sirs.

(The Magistrate and Notary exit into Valère's house.)

SGANARELLE
Now then, I'll reveal
Some secrets to you.

(They retire to the back of the stage.)

Scene 8

Léonor, Sganarelle, Ariste, Lisette.

LÉONOR
Oh, what a grim ordeal!
I find those young men tiresome, one and all.
On their account, I slipped away from the ball.

LISETTE
They all try hard to please you, and be engaging.

LÉONOR
Nevertheless, I find their talk enraging;
I'd rather hear the simplest common sense
Than all that empty prattle they dispense.
They think their blond wigs dazzle every eye,
And that they're fearfully witty when they try

77

To tease one, in a bright, malicious fashion,
About the limits of an old man's passion.
But I prefer an old man's kindly zeal
To the giddy transports young men claim to feel.
Ah! Don't I see—?

SGANARELLE

(To Ariste:)
    Well, Brother, now you know. *(Perceiving Léonor)*
But look! She's coming, with her maid in tow.

ARISTE

Léonor, I am not angry, but I'm pained:
You know your freedom's never been constrained,
And that you've long been promised, on my part,
Full liberty in matters of the heart.
Yet, as if doubtful that I would approve,
You've gone behind my back to pledge your love.
I don't regret my leniency, but such
Mistrustful conduct hurts me very much,
And what you've done is not a fair return
For my affection and my warm concern.

LÉONOR

I cannot guess to what your words refer;
My feelings, though, are what they always were,
And my regard for you is firm and strong.
I could not love another, and do you wrong.
If you would see my chief wish satisfied,
Say that tomorrow I may be your bride.

ARISTE

Then, Brother, on what foundation did you base—?

SGANARELLE

What! Didn't you come, just now, from Valère's place?
Didn't you tell your sister, just today,
That, a year ago, he stole your heart away?

LÉONOR

Tell me, who took the trouble to devise
Such tales about me, and spin such pretty lies?

Scene 9

Isabelle, Valère, the Magistrate, the Notary, Ergaste, Lisette, Léonor,
Sganarelle, Ariste.

ISABELLE

Sister, I fear I've taken liberties
With your good name; will you forgive me, please?
Under the pressure of a sudden crisis
I've stooped, today, to certain low devices:
By your example I am put to shame;
But fortune did not treat us both the same.
(To Sganarelle:)
Sir, I shall offer no apologies tò you;
It is a service, not a wrong, I do you.
The heavens did not design us to be wed:
I felt unworthy of you, and instead
Of making you an undeserving wife,
I chose another man to share my life.

VALÈRE

(To Sganarelle:)
I count it, sir, my greatest joy and pride
That from your hands I have received my bride.

ARISTE

Best take this quietly, Brother; your own extreme
Behavior forced these two to plot and scheme,
And it will be your sad lot, I foresee,
To be a dupe who gets no sympathy.

LISETTE

Well, I'm delighted. This clever trick's a just
Reward for his suspicion and mistrust.

LÉONOR

I'm not sure that their trick deserves applause,
But I can't blame them, for they had good cause.

ERGASTE

He's a born cuckold, and lucky to get out
Of marriage before his horns began to sprout.

SGANARELLE

(Emerging from his stupefaction:)
No, I can't fathom it; I'm overcome;
Such treachery is too deep for me to plumb;
I can't believe that Satan himself could be
As wicked as this jade has been to me.
I would have sworn she could not do amiss;
Let no man trust a woman, after this!
The best of them are guileful and perverse;
Their breed was made to be creation's curse.
The Devil take them all! I hereby sever
Relations with their faithless sex forever.

ERGASTE

Good.

ARISTE

Come to my house, friends. Tomorrow we'll assuage,
As best we can, my brother's pain and rage.

LISETTE

(To the audience:)
D'you know any churlish husbands? If you do,
Send them to us: We'll teach them a thing or two.

END OF PLAY

The Imaginary Cuckold, or Sganarelle

Introduction

This little comedy was first presented by Molière's troupe on May 28, 1660. It was at once a hit, and during the "dead season" of summer, despite the absence of the court and the exodus of the rich and fashionable, it played to full houses. By the end of the year, it had been done a remarkable thirty-four times at the Petit-Bourbon, and privately performed a half dozen times for Cardinal Mazarin or the delighted king. One enthusiast, a man named Neufvillenaine, saw it often enough to memorize the dialogue and to publish, in Molière's honor, a pirated edition of the play. During Molière's lifetime, *Sganarelle* was offered by his company every year, and in all had more performances than any other of his works, with second honors going to *The School for Husbands.*

 The Imaginary Cuckold, or Sganarelle has many qualities that may be seen as deriving from the tradition—then two centuries old—of the one-act French farce. Farce is concerned with standard comic types at the mercy of absurd situations, and surely such figures as the young lovers Célie and Lélie, or the earthy and insolent servant Gros-René, are as simple and generic as possible. The plot is a fast-developing imbroglio that, having built to a peak of confusion, concludes with a brisk and convenient dénouement. It is loaded with coincidences and ludicrous misunderstandings. There is a certain amount of vulgar language in *Sganarelle,* and though it is scarcely a knockabout piece, it contains a fair bit of physical comedy: The parallel swoons of Célie and Lélie, Sganarelle's examination of Célie's bosom, his avoidances of Lélie in Scene 9, his bold advances and craven retreats in Scene Twenty-One.

In all these ways, *Sganarelle* partakes of the flavor, rhythm and general makeup of farce. Yet, having said that, one must begin at once to qualify. The rudimentary persons of farce are commonly subordinate to a hectic plot, and seem to be manipulated by it; but that is not quite the case here. Lélie, Célie, Sganarelle and his wife are all in some degree mistrustful of their mates or beloveds before they encounter "proof" of inconstancy; and in Scene Twenty-Two, when all has been explained away, we see Sganarelle and his wife still clinging to their doubts of one another. It is the characters, then, who spin the plot of *Sganarelle* with their want of faith; and though the play is far from philosophical, it rests upon thoughts about suspicion, evidence and trust which will surface more importantly in *Tartuffe.*

Above all, it is the title character (originally played by Molière himself) who cannot be seen as a mere cog in the plot machinery. Rather, it is the business of much of the plot to reveal the comic riches of his nature. In his most appealing aspect, Sganarelle is a Falstaffian figure who loves life and does not think much of death, heroic or otherwise. But he is also a prodigy of self-absorption. As one commentator observes, he is "hard on others, soft on himself," and he continually oscillates between blustering self-assertion and timid recoil. So insulated is he that, in these repeated waverings, he seems like a shadow boxer afraid of his shadow. The play variously shows us the extent of his egoism: he is blithely callous when Célie is thought to be dying; he often thinks himself alone when he is not; and when Célie berates the absent Lélie, he believes that she is uttering *his* grievance. He expresses his complex nature in three distinct voices. One voice is that of a crudely voluble bourgeois who, when addressing his wife, is consistently brutal. The second voice is clownishly ironic, and is especially heard in Scene Six where, unable to make a plain statement of his suspicions, he resorts to a buffoonery that has the effect of simultaneous accusation and retraction. The third voice belongs to Sganarelle the fantasist, who dramatizes his supposed disgrace (Scene 9) and his temporary courage (Scene Twenty-One) in stilted soliloquies suggestive of tragic theater. Sganarelle, in short, is a character diversely revealed, who anticipates all those later Molière heroes (Arnolphe, Alceste) who are self-centered, self-assertive, ill-adjusted and victimized by their own obsessive notions.

"One would call it a farce," a French critic writes of *Sganarelle*, "if it were not written in verse." Certainly it is true that Molière's third verse comedy, by wedding broad effects to a now polished poetic technique, makes it hard to speak confidently of low comedy or high; it is somewhat as if a comic strip had been rendered in oils. Much of what might have been expressed by physical violence—Gorgibus's recurrent urge to thrash his daughter, the Punch-and-Judy relationship of Sganarelle and his wife—is realized instead on the verbal plane, a plane on which Célie's maid has leisure to sketch a delectable self-portrait (Scene Two), and Sganarelle to display his mood swings in a lengthy monologue. The sixty-eight-line speech in which he does so constitutes the whole of Scene Seventeen, which was called *"la belle scène"* in Molière's day. It is not hard to see why mid-eighteenth-century editors of Molière, associating well-turned and sustained alexandrines with high comedy, divided *Sganarelle* into three acts, cutting into the play at the two scene endings (Scenes Six and Seventeen) that leave the stage empty.

It was a mistake, of course, to dignify *Sganarelle* with such stately movement; the piece should be done continuously and at a good clip, as Molière intended and as La Grange's edition (1682) makes plain. And M. Neufvillenaine's descriptions of Molière in the title role, which he played without a mask, make it clear that a certain amount of broad clowning is authorized. "No one," says Neufvillenaine, "was ever better at making and unmaking his face, and it is safe to say that in the course of this play he transforms his features more than twenty times . . . his pantomime gives rise to endless bursts of applause." But if some present-day director of *Sganarelle* honors Molière's precedent as to pace and acting style, let him also honor the artful *spoken-ness* of this comedy, and make sure that the verse dialogue is nowhere sacrificed to irrelevant horseplay and hubbub. Unless the lines are well said and clearly heard, there will be a loss of wit and timing, of character portrayal, and even of plot. This is particularly true toward the end of the play, where the four principals converge, each speaking out of a different—or differently weighted—misunderstanding of the situation. Sganarelle thinks that he is a cuckold and that his wife is in love with Lélie; Lélie thinks that Célie, his betrothed, has jilted him and married Sganarelle; Célie thinks that her fiancé, Lélie, has betrayed her with Sganarelle's wife; and Sganarelle's wife thinks that her husband is enamored of Célie. Such interplay of strong delusions can challenge the imaginative agility of an audience, and so give pleasure; or if badly performed, it can be merely chaotic, which does not amuse for long.

Gorgibus, in the fourth speech of the play, makes mention of a number of books that were very well known in Molière's century. *Clélie* (1654–1660) was a wildly popular sentimental novel by Madeleine de Scudéry. The *Quatrains* of the magistrate Guy du Faur de Pibrac (d. 1584) and the *Tablettes de la vie et de la mort* of the historian Pierre Matthieu (d. 1621), were edifying texts deemed essential to the education of the young. The *Guide des pêcheurs* was an ascetic devotional book by a Spanish Dominican, Luis of Granada (d. 1588). I have made a few trivial changes in the text, for ease of speaking or of understanding. For example, Célie's maid says in Scene Two, "God rest my poor Martin," but I thought that "God rest my dear dead Jacques" would be easier for an American actress to say. And in the same character's last speech (Scene Twenty-Two), I have substituted "a little pill / Of common sense" for the original's *"peu d'ellébore,"* because folk medicine no longer speaks, as it did in the Middle Ages, of hellebore as a cure for madness.

—RW

Cummington, Massachusetts, 1993

Characters

GORGIBUS (gor-gee-BOOSE), a middle-class Parisian

CÉLIE (say-LEE), his daughter

LÉLIE (lay-LEE), a young man in love with Célie

GROS-RENÉ (grow-ra-NAY), Lélie's valet

SGANARELLE (skan-a-RELL), a Parisian bourgeois and an imaginary cuckold

SGANARELLE'S WIFE

VILLEBREQUIN (veal-breck-KAN), father of Valère, to whom Célie is promised

CÉLIE'S MAID

A MALE RELATIVE OF SGANARELLE'S WIFE

The Scene

A residential square in Paris.

Scene 1

Gorgibus, Célie, Célie's Maid.

CÉLIE
(Entering in tears, followed by her father.)
No, no! My heart will never consent to this.

GORGIBUS
What do I hear you say, my saucy miss?
Dare you oppose my wishes, and dispute
A parent's power, which is absolute?
D'you hope to sway, by foolish arguments,
Your father's judgment and mature good sense?
Which of us, in our household, has dominion?
And is it you or I, in your opinion,
Who knows what's best for you, you silly child?

By Heaven, be careful not to get me riled,
Or you'll have cause to know, this very minute,
Whether my arm still has some muscle in it.
You'd better cease your grumbling, Miss Contrary,
And accept the man I've picked for you to marry.
You tell me that I know too little of him,
And should have asked you first if you could love him:
Well, knowing his fortune, which is large indeed,
What other information do I need?
And as for love, does not a husband who
Has twenty thousand ducats appeal to you?
Whatever he's like, a man as rich as he
Is a perfect gentleman, I'll guarantee.

CÉLIE

Alas!

GORGIBUS

Well, well. "Alas," you tell me, eh?
What a very fine "alas" this girl can say!
Take care, now; if you make me hit the ceiling,
I'll give you cause to say "alas"—with feeling!
This is what comes, young lady, of your addiction
To all these volumes of romantic fiction;
Your head is full of amorous rigmarole,
And you care more for *Clélie* than for your soul.
Such trashy books, I tell you, should be flung
In the fire, because they much corrupt the young.
Instead of such insidious poppycock,
Go read Matthieu, or the *Quatrains* of Pibrac—
Instructive literature that's sound and wise
And full of maxims you should memorize.
Read, too, the *Sinner's Guide*; no book can give

A young girl better advice on how to live.
Had such books been your only reading, you'd
Have learned a more obedient attitude.

CÉLIE

But, Father! Can you mean for me to be
False to the love I've promised to Lélie?
A girl can't wed, I know, at her own whim;
But you yourself, sir, pledged my hand to him.

GORGIBUS

What if I did? I now transfer my pledge
To another man, whose wealth gives him the edge.
Lélie's a handsome fellow, but do learn
That a suitor's purse should be your first concern,
That gold can make the ugliest mate seem fair,
And that, without it, life's a sad affair.
You don't much like Valère, I know; but still,
Though the lover may not please you, the husband will.
That sweet word *spouse* can cause the heart to soften,
And love is born of marriage, very often.
But I'm a fool to argue and persuade,
When a father should command, and be obeyed!
Let's have no more, please, of your insolence,
And spare me your alases and laments.
My future son-in-law will call tonight;
Be sure, be very sure, to treat him right:
If you dare to be unwelcoming and cold,
I'll . . . Well, I'll say no more. Do as you're told.

93

Scene 2

Célie, Célie's Maid.

MAID

Dear Mistress, what possesses you to spurn
The thing for which so many women yearn—
To greet a marriage offer with streaming eyes,
And balk at saying yes to such a prize?
If only someone asked my hand, there'd be
No need to press the matter, believe you me,
And I'd not find that "yes" was hard to say:
I'd blurt a dozen yesses, right away.
Your little brother's tutor, who comes around
To hear his daily lessons, was very sound
When, telling us of Nature's great design,
He said that woman is like the ivy vine,
Which, clinging to its oak, grows lush and tall,
But, lacking that support, can't thrive at all.
No truer words were ever spoken, ma'am,
As well I know, poor sinner that I am.
God rest my dear dead Jacques! Before he died,
My eye was merry, my heart was satisfied,
My cheeks were rosy and my body plump,
And now I'm nothing but a sad old frump.
Back in those sweet days when I had a man,
I slept all winter without a warming pan;
Small need there was to spread my sheets to dry!
But now I shiver even in July.
Believe me, dearest Mistress, there's nothing quite
Like having a husband next to you at night,
If only for the cozy thought that he's
Nearby to say, "God bless you," when you sneeze.

CÉLIE

Would you have me jilt my dear Lélie, and wed
This ugly-looking man Valère instead?

MAID

Well, your Lélie's a blockhead, in my view,
To take so long a trip away from you,
And his extended absence makes me start
To wonder if he's had a change of heart.

CÉLIE

(Showing her a locket containing the portrait of Lélie:)
No, I'll not entertain that dire conjecture.
Look at the noble features in this picture;
They speak to me of love that shall not die.
I can't believe such lineaments could lie,
And since it's he whose face is imaged here,
I know my love will ever hold me dear.

MAID

He has a faithful lover's face, that's true,
And you're quite right to love him as you do.

CÉLIE

But what if I'm forced . . . Oh, hold me!

(She drops Lélie's portrait.)

MAID

(Supporting Célie as she swoons:)
                    Madam, pray,
What ails you? . . . Heavens! She's fainted dead away!
Help, someone! Hurry!

Scene 3

Célie, Sganarelle, Célie's Maid.

SGANARELLE

What's up? Did I hear you call?

MAID

Oh, sir, my lady's dying.

SGANARELLE

Is that all?
You screamed as though all Hell had reared its head.
Let's have a look at her. Madam, are you dead?
Huh! She says nothing.

MAID

I'll go fetch someone who
Will help to carry her. Hold her, I beg of you.

Scene 4

Célie, Sganarelle, Sganarelle's Wife.

SGANARELLE
(Supporting Célie, and passing his hand over her bosom:)
She's cold all over; is that a proof of death?
I'll watch her lips, to see if she takes a breath.
My word! I can't be sure, but it seems to me
That her mouth shows signs of life.

WIFE
(Looking down from a window:)
Oh! What do I see?

My husband and some woman . . . I'll slip downstairs
And catch that cheating rascal unawares.

SGANARELLE
(To a man whom the Maid has brought in:)
Come, we must get her help without delay;
It would be wrong of her to pass away.
The other world's a stupid place to go
When everything's so pleasant here below.

Scene 5

Sganarelle's Wife alone.

WIFE
Well, he has suddenly vanished from this place,
And I can't learn the full facts of the case;
But the little I saw has left no room for doubt:
The man's a traitor, and I have found him out.
I now well understand the chilly fashion
Of his responses to my wifely passion:
He saves his hugs for other women, the swine,
And feeds their appetites while starving mine.
Well, that's how husbands are: For them, the joy
Of lawful wedded love soon starts to cloy.
At first they think it wondrous and sublime,
And fervently adore us, but in time
They weary of our kisses, and start to roam,
Bestowing elsewhere what belongs at home.
O for a law that would allow us women
To change our husbands as we change our linen!
What a boon for wives! And I know many a one
Who'd gladly do it if it could be done.

(Picking up the portrait dropped by Célie:)
But what's this locket, which chance drops at my feet?
The enamel's charming, the engraving neat.
I'll open it.

Scene 6

Sganarelle, Sganarelle's Wife.

SGANARELLE

(Thinking himself alone:)
    Was she dead? No, not a bit
She'd only fainted, and soon came out of it.
But I see my wife.

WIFE

(Thinking herself alone:)
    Oh, my! It's a miniature!
What a handsome man! What lifelike portraiture!

SGANARELLE

(Aside, as he looks over his wife's shoulder:)
What is she so absorbed in looking at?
A portrait, eh? I don't much care for that.
A dark suspicion takes possession of me.

WIFE

(Not noticing her husband:)
I've never laid eyes upon a thing so lovely.
The workmanship's more precious than the gold.
And it smells so fragrant!

SGANARELLE

(*Aside:*)
             So, I was right! Behold,
She's kissing it!

WIFE

(*Still unaware of her husband:*)
             I confess that I would be
Ravished if such a man paid court to me,
And that, if his sweet pleadings should persist,
My virtue might not manage to resist.
Ah, why can't I have a mate thus nobly made,
Instead of the bald clown—

SGANARELLE

(*Snatching away the portrait:*)
             Hold on, you jade!
I've caught you in the act. You dare defame
Your husband, and asperse his honored name.
So then, milady, in your considered view,
Milord is not quite good enough for you!
Well, by the Devil (and may the Devil take you),
What better gift than me could Heaven make you?
Can you perceive in me a single flaw?
This figure, which the world regards with awe,
This face, which wakens love in each beholder
And makes a thousand beauties sigh and smolder,
Don't these, and all my other charms, provide
A feast with which you should be satisfied?
Or does a tasty husband not suffice,
So that you need a gallant, for added spice?

WIFE

I see right through your sly buffooneries.
You hope thereby to—

SGANARELLE

No evasions, please.
The case is proved, and here in my possession
Is the clearest evidence of your transgression.

WIFE

See here: My anger is already strong,
Without your doing me a second wrong.
Give back my locket, and keep your tongue in check.
What do you mean—

SGANARELLE

I mean to wring your neck.
Oh, how I wish the rogue who's pictured here
Were in my clutches!

WIFE

What for?

SGANARELLE

Why, nothing, dear!
I'm wrong to be resentful, and my brow
Should thank you for the gifts it's wearing now.
(*Looking at Lélie's portrait:*)
Yes, there he is, your pretty boy, your pet,
The spark by whom your secret fire was set,
The wretch with whom . . .

WIFE

With whom . . . Go on. What's next?

SGANARELLE

With whom, I say . . . and it makes me deeply vexed.

WIFE

What is this drunken idiot trying to say?

SGANARELLE

You take my meaning, strumpet. It's plain as day.
My name's no longer Sganarelle, and folk
Will dub me Mister Staghorn, for a joke.
You've made me lose my honor; but when I'm through,
I shall have made you lose a tooth or two.

WIFE

How dare you speak to me so threateningly?

SGANARELLE

How dare you play such wicked tricks on me?

WIFE

What wicked tricks? Talk plainly. Spell it out.

SGANARELLE

Ah, no, I've nothing to be sore about!
What does it matter if people laugh and stare
At the buck's antlers you have made me wear?

WIFE

So, having wronged me by a grave offense—
The crime a married woman most resents—
You seek now to forestall my rage by feigning
A righteous wrath, and clownishly complaining!
I've never seen so insolent a ruse:
The one you've sinned against, you dare accuse.

SGANARELLE

My! Judging by the haughty speech you've made me,
One might mistake you for a virtuous lady!

WIFE

Go on, pursue your mistresses, address them
With tender words, and lovingly caress them:
But let me have my locket, you lustful ape.

(She snatches the portrait from him, and flees.)

SGANARELLE

(Running after her:)
I'll get that back, don't worry . . . you shan't escape.

Scene 7

Lélie, Gros-René.

GROS-RENÉ

We're home at last. But now, sir, if you'll hear me,
I'd like to pose to you a little query.

LÉLIE

Well, ask it.

GROS-RENÉ

        Are you possessed, sir, by some devil,
So that you're not worn out by all this travel?
For eight whole days we've galloped, sir; from dawn
To dusk we've spurred our spavined horses on,
And been so tossed and jolted by their pace
That all my bones feel bruised and out of place,
Not to forget a blister hot as flame
That pains me in a spot I shall not name:
Yet you, once here, rush out on eager feet
Without a moment's rest, or a bite to eat.

LÉLIE

Our swift return was wholly necessary.
I'd heard dire news that Célie soon might marry;
You know I love her; I now must go in haste
And learn on what that dread report was based.

GROS-RENÉ

Yes, but you need a good square meal, sir, ere
You sally forth to fathom this affair;
'Twill fortify your heart, you may be sure,
To bear whatever shocks it must endure.
That's how it is with me; when I haven't eaten,
The smallest setback leaves me crushed and beaten;
But when my belly's full, my soul is strong,
And the worst mischance can't trouble me for long.
Be wise, then: Stuff yourself, and that will steel you
Against such bitter blows as fate may deal you;
Moreover, make your heart immune to woe
By downing twenty cups of wine or so.

LÉLIE

No, I can't eat.

GROS-RENÉ

(Sotto voce, aside:)
        If I don't eat soon, I'll die!
(Aloud:)
Your dinner could be served in the wink of an eye.

LÉLIE

Be still, I tell you.

GROS-RENÉ
How cruel! How unkind!

LÉLIE

It's worry, and not hunger, that's on my mind.

GROS-RENÉ

I'm hungry, sir, and it worries me to learn
That a foolish passion is your sole concern.

LÉLIE

Let me seek news of her whom I adore;
Go eat, if you wish, and pester me no more.

GROS-RENÉ

I shall not question such a sound command.

Scene 8

Lélie alone.

LÉLIE

No, no, I've let my fears get out of hand;
Her father's solemn promise, and her demure
Avowals of love should make my hopes secure.

Scene 9

Sganarelle, Lélie.

SGANARELLE

(Not seeing Lélie, and holding the portrait in his hands:)
I've got it back, and I'll study now the face
Of the scoundrel who's the cause of my disgrace . . .
No, I don't know him.

LÉLIE

(Aside:)

Great heavens! What have I seen?
Is that my portrait? What can this possibly mean?

SGANARELLE

(Not seeing Lélie.)
Alas, poor Sganarelle, your once proud name
Is doomed to suffer mockery and shame!
Henceforth . . .

(Noticing that Lélie is looking at him, he turns away.)

LÉLIE

(Aside:)

'Twill cause my faith in her to waver,
If she has parted with the gift I gave her.

SGANARELLE

(Aside:)
Henceforth you shall be scorned by all you meet;
They'll point two fingers at you in the street,
And balladeers will jest about the horrid
Growths that a witch has planted on your forehead!

LÉLIE

(Aside:)
Could I be wrong?

SGANARELLE

(Aside:)

How could you, vicious wife,
Make me a cuckold in my prime of life?
Why, when your mate's well favored, spry and dapper,
Were you attracted to this whippersnapper?

LÉLIE

(Aside, as he once more looks at the portrait in Sganarelle's hands:)
No, it's my portrait, just as I surmised.

SGANARELLE

(Aside, turning his back to Lélie:)
That man is nosy.

LÉLIE

(Aside:)
      I'm utterly surprised.

SGANARELLE

(Aside:)
What does he want?

LÉLIE

(Aside:)
      I'll speak to him. *(To Sganarelle)* If I may . . .
(Sganarelle starts moving away.)
Wait! Just one word.

SGANARELLE

(Aside, still moving away:)
      What is it he wants to say?

LÉLIE

I should be grateful if you told me how
You acquired the portrait that you're holding now.

SGANARELLE

(Aside:)
Why does he want to know? But let me see . . .
(He studies Lélie and the portrait which he is holding:)

Ah! Now his feverish air makes sense to me!
This clarifies his actions very nicely.
I've found my man—or my wife's man, more precisely.

LÉLIE

Relieve my mind, and tell me from whose hand—

SGANARELLE

What makes you ask, I now well understand.
This pretty locket, in which your face is painted,
I got from one with whom you're well acquainted;
And I am well aware, sir, of your dealings
With her, and of your ardent mutual feelings.
I don't know if I have the honor, sir,
Of being known to you, by way of her,
But do me the honor to pursue no more
A love which, as her husband, I deplore.
When sacred marriage vows are lightly broken—

LÉLIE

What! She, you say, from whom you got this token—

SGANARELLE

Is my wife, and I'm her husband.

LÉLIE

Her husband? You?

SGANARELLE

Yes, I'm her husband, and her victim, too.
You know my grievance, which I'm off to share
With all her kinfolk.

Scene 10

Lélie, alone.

LÉLIE
Oh, this is hard to bear!
Those rumors that I heard were truthful, then;
She's married, and to the ugliest of men!
Ah, traitress, even if you hadn't sworn
Eternal love to me, you ought in scorn
To have refused that loutish fellow's suit,
And chosen me instead of such a brute.
Yes, faithless woman . . . But now this bitter wrong,
And the strains of traveling so far and long,
Are all at once too much for me; they make
My heart grow feeble and my body quake.

Scene 11

Lélie, Sganarelle's Wife.

WIFE
(Thinking herself alone at first, then perceiving Lélie:)
That traitor took my . . . Sir, are you ill, perhaps?
You look to me as if you might collapse.

LÉLIE
I've had a sudden dizzy spell, I fear.

WIFE
It wouldn't do for you to faint out here.
Come into my house until it passes, do.

LÉLIE

I'll accept your kindness, for a moment or two.

Scene 12

Sganarelle, a male Relative of Sganarelle's Wife.

RELATIVE

Husbands do well to guard their honor; but surely
You bring these charges rather prematurely.
You're very far, dear boy, from having built
A solid case which demonstrates her guilt.
One shouldn't accuse a wife of this offense
Without strong proof and clinching evidence.

SGANARELLE

One has to catch her clinching, as it were.

RELATIVE

By judging hastily, we often err.
Who knows how she acquired that portrait? Can
You prove that she has ever met that man?
Clear up those questions; then, if you're right, we'll be
The first to punish her iniquity.

Scene 13

Sganarelle alone.

SGANARELLE

Well said: One should be cautious in such cases,
And take things slowly. Perhaps there was no basis

109

For the hornish visions that I had just now,
And all that nervous sweat upon my brow.
That portrait, after all, which so dismayed me,
Gives me no certain proof that she's betrayed me.
I'll be more careful . . .

Scene 14

Sganarelle, Sganarelle's Wife showing Lélie to her door, Lélie.

SGANARELLE

(*Aside:*)
      What's this? My blood runs cold!
It's no mere portrait that I now behold;
Look, there he is—the man himself, in person.

WIFE

Stay, sir, and rest, lest your condition worsen.
If you leave so soon, that seizure may return.

LÉLIE

No, no, I thank you for your kind concern,
And for your timely help in my distress.

SGANARELLE

(*Aside:*)
What help the trollop gave him, I can guess!

(*Sganarelle's Wife retires into her house.*)

Scene 15

Sganarelle, Lélie.

SGANARELLE

(Aside:)
He's noticed me; let's see what he dares to say.

LÉLIE

(Aside:)
Ah, there's that creature, vile in every way . . .
But no, in fairness I must curb my hate,
And blame my woes on nothing but my fate.
I shall but envy him his happy lot.
(Approaching Sganarelle:)
Ah, lucky man! What a splendid wife you've got!

Scene 16

Sganarelle, Célie at her window, seeing the departing Lélie.

SGANARELLE

(Alone:)
Well, that was unambiguous! Now I know.
His brutal frankness stuns me; it's as though
A pair of horns had started from my head.
(Looking in the direction in which Lélie has gone:)
Such conduct, sir, is not at all well bred!

CÉLIE

(Aside, as she enters:)
I can't believe it. Just now I saw Lélie;
But why was his return concealed from me?

SGANARELLE

(*Not seeing Célie:*)
"Ah, lucky man! What a splendid wife you've got!"
No, luckless me, to have wed a sly cocotte
Whose guilty passion, now revealed, has led
To my disgrace, and left me cuckolded!
As for her lover—after what he'd done,
Why did I stand there like a simpleton
And let him go? I should have smashed his hat,
Thrown mud upon his cloak, and after that
Roused all the neighborhood against that thief
Of honor, to give my fury some relief.

(*During this speech of Sganarelle's, Célie approaches bit by bit and waits for his transport to end, so that she may speak to him.*)

CÉLIE

(*To Sganarelle:*)
If I may ask, how is it that you know
The man who spoke to you a moment ago?

SGANARELLE

Alas, I do not know the man, not I;
It's my wife who knows him.

CÉLIE

You seem much troubled. Why?

SGANARELLE

My sorrow, I assure you, is not groundless;
I must lament, because my woe is boundless.

CÉLIE

What can have caused you so extreme a pain?

SGANARELLE

It's of no piddling thing that I complain,
And surely there's no man alive who in
My place would fail to feel a deep chagrin.
I am the model of a luckless spouse.
Poor Sganarelle, the honor of your house
Is lost! But honor's nothing to the shame
Of having been deprived of my good name.

CÉLIE

But how?

SGANARELLE

In plain terms, madam, that popinjay
Has made a cuckold of me, and today
These eyes of mine have witnessed shocking proof
That he meets my wife beneath my very roof.

CÉLIE

The man who just now—

SGANARELLE

Yes, he's filched my honor.
My wife adores him, and he dotes upon her.

CÉLIE

I thought so! He returned in secrecy
So as to hide a base deceit from me;
I trembled when I saw him, for I knew
By instinct what has proven all too true.

SGANARELLE

It's very good of you to take my part:
Not everybody has so kind a heart;

And some will view my martyrdom hereafter
Not with compassion but with mocking laughter.

CÉLIE

(*Addressing the absent Lélie:*)
What darker deed than yours could one commit?
What vengeance could suffice to punish it?
After this crime, too dreadful to forgive,
Have you not forfeited the right to live?
Gods! Can such vileness be?

SGANARELLE

Alas, it can.

CÉLIE

O traitor! Scoundrel! False and faithless man!

SGANARELLE

What a generous soul!

CÉLIE

No, no, Hell cannot offer
Such agonies as you deserve to suffer!

SGANARELLE

What eloquence!

CÉLIE

To think that you'd deceive
A heart so pure, devoted and naive!

SGANARELLE

Well said!

CÉLIE

A guiltless heart which never earned
The fate of being thus betrayed and spurned!

SGANARELLE

Too true.

CÉLIE

A heart . . . but ah, I'm overcome
By mortal sorrow, and am stricken dumb.

SGANARELLE

It moves me deeply that my plight should touch
You so, dear lady; but do not grieve too much.

CÉLIE

Don't dream, however, that I shall be content
With sad reproaches and with vain lament:
I crave revenge, and I shall quickly take it;
That's my resolve, and nothing now can shake it.

Scene 17

Sganarelle alone.

SGANARELLE

May Heaven keep her safe from harm! I find
Her wish to avenge me very sweet and kind.
Indeed, her generous anger at my plight
Prompts me to rouse myself, and show some fight,
For any man who suffers such affronts

Without a word is but a craven dunce.
Come then! I'll track him down, and with a brave
Resolve avenge myself upon the knave.
I'll teach you, churl, to laugh at folks' expense,
And cuckold people with such insolence!
(*Having taken several steps, he comes back again.*)
But not so fast; let's wait a bit. Good gracious,
That fellow looks hot-blooded and pugnacious,
And he might leave his mark, should I attack,
Not merely on my brow but on my back.
I can't stand folk who have a violent streak,
And those I love are peaceable and meek;
I strike no man, for men can turn and hurt you,
And mild good nature is my greatest virtue.
And yet my honor says to me that I
Must take revenge for this affront, or die:
Well, rave on, dearest Honor, talk your fill;
I won't obey you; damn me if I will!
When I have played the hero, and for reward
Have had my guts impaled upon a sword,
And gossips tell my death on every corner,
Will you be happy then, my dearest Honor?
The grave's a dreary domicile, I'm told,
And just the place to catch one's death of cold,
And as for me, I think, when all is said,
It's better to be cuckolded than dead.
What harm does it do a fellow? Does it bow
His legs, or spoil his figure, I'd like to know?
A curse on the demented person who
First thought of such a stupid bugaboo,
And tied the honor of a man to what
His wife may do, if she's a fickle slut.
The guilty one should pay in such a case;
Why must our honor suffer in her place?

The wrongs that others do are charged to us,
And if our spouses prove adulterous
We husbands are to shoulder all the blame:
They're shameless, and it's we who bear the shame!
This is a rank injustice, and should be
Corrected by some statute or decree.
Aren't there sufficient woes and sufferings
That plague us in the normal course of things—
Don't sickness, lawsuits, hunger, thirst and strife
Sufficiently beset us in this life—
Without our adding to them by conceiving
Another and quite baseless cause for grieving?
Away with this chimera and its fears;
I'll groan no more, and shed no further tears.
If my wife's done wrong, it's she who should lament;
Why should I weep, when I am innocent?
In any case, it comforts me to be
A member of a wide fraternity,
For many husbands nowadays, I've heard,
When their wives cheat them, never say a word.
I'll pick no quarrel, then, but wisely stifle
My ire at what is, after all, a trifle.
If I don't seek vengeance, people may deride me,
But I'd look sillier with a sword inside me.
(Placing his hand on his breast:)
And yet I feel the stirrings of a passion
Which urges me to act in manly fashion:
Yes, I'm enraged; enough of cowardice;
I'll make that low seducer pay for this:
As my first move, I'll let the whole town know
That he's sleeping with my wife, the so-and-so.

Scene 18

Gorgibus, Célie, Célie's Maid.

CÉLIE

Yes, Father, I bow to your authority:
Do as you wish, sir, with my hand and me,
And let the marriage contract soon be signed;
I do my duty with a willing mind.
I have renounced my former feelings, and
In all things shall obey your least command.

GORGIBUS

Ah! That's the kind of talk I like to hear.
By Jove, your words delight me so, my dear,
That these old legs might caper and cavort
If folk weren't near to see me and make sport.
Come here, my daughter; come to my embrace.
In such behavior there is no disgrace;
A father's free to give his daughter a kiss
Without the neighbors taking it amiss.
Haha! It makes me ten years younger to
Have heard such sweet, submissive words from you.

Scene 19

Célie, Célie's Maid.

MAID

Your change of mind astounds me.

CÉLIE

When I apprise
You of the facts, you'll say that I've been wise.

MAID

Perhaps I will.

CÉLIE

The fact is that Lélie
Has played me false; without informing me
Of his return, he—

MAID

Here he comes, however.

Scene 20

Lélie, Célie, Célie's Maid.

LÉLIE

Before I take my leave of you forever,
I wish to tell you how my heart resents—

CÉLIE

How can you face me now? What impudence!

LÉLIE

I see; I'm impudent! And I'd be a beast
To question your decision in the least!
Be happy, then, with this most brilliant man
You've chosen, and forget me if you can.

CÉLIE

I mean to be happy, traitor; and my chief
Desire is that my joy should cause you grief.

LÉLIE

What have I done, pray, to enrage you so?

CÉLIE

Ha! What have you done? As if you didn't know.

Scene 21

Célie, Lélie, Sganarelle (armed from head to foot), Célie's Maid.

SGANARELLE

War, bloody war! I warn the thief who dared
To steal my honor, that war is now declared!

CÉLIE

(To Lélie, pointing to Sganarelle:)
Look, there's my answer; you know the man, of course.

LÉLIE

Ah, yes—

CÉLIE

That sight should cause you deep remorse.

LÉLIE

The sight of him should make your cheeks turn red.

SGANARELLE

(Aside:)
My anger now has gathered to a head;

My courage is in full arousal, too;
And if I find him, carnage will ensue.
Yes, he must perish; nothing shall prevent it;
I've sworn to slay the villain, and I meant it.
(With sword half drawn, he approaches Lélie.)
I'll cleave his heart with one stupendous blow—

LÉLIE

(Turning around.)
What foe are you seeking?

SGANARELLE

None; I have no foe.

LÉLIE

Then why this armor?

SGANARELLE

It's something that I wear
In case of rain.
(Aside:)
Oh, it would be a rare
Pleasure to kill him! Come now, my heart, be firm.

LÉLIE

(Turning around again.)
Eh?

SGANARELLE

I said nothing.
(Aside, after slapping his face several times to rouse his initiative:)
Oh, you spineless worm!
You hateful coward!

CÉLIE

His presence here gives rise
To guilty thoughts, and so he offends your eyes.

LÉLIE

Yes, when I look at him I see your guilt;
How could you so unconscionably jilt
A faithful lover, who earned no such rebuff?

SGANARELLE

(Aside:)
Oh, for some courage!

CÉLIE

Traitor, I've heard enough!
Such brazen insolence I won't abide.

SGANARELLE

(Aside:)
Hark, Sganarelle, the lady is on your side!
Take heart, my boy, let's see some fire and vim.
Forward! And make a bold attack on him,
And bravely kill him while his back is turned.

LÉLIE

(Taking two or three aimless steps, which cause Sganarelle, who was
approaching to kill him, to retreat.)
Since all my honest words are fiercely spurned,
I'll flatter you, and say that you've displayed
Sublime good taste in the choice your heart has made.

CÉLIE

My choice is sound, and the world can but commend it.

LÉLIE

You have no choice, alas, but to defend it.

SGANARELLE

She's right indeed, sir, to defend my cause.
The thing you've done breaks all the moral laws:
You've wronged me, and were I not so self-controlled,
A scene of butchery might now unfold.

LÉLIE

Why this grim threat? Of what am I accused?

SGANARELLE

Enough; you well know how I've been abused;
Conscience should tell you that by Heaven's decree
My wife is my exclusive property,
And that to act as if you owned her, too,
Is not at all a Christian thing to do.

LÉLIE

It's quite ridiculous, this charge you make;
But put your fears to rest, for Heaven's sake:
Your wife is yours, and I shan't appropriate her.

CÉLIE

How smoothly you dissimulate, you traitor!

LÉLIE

What! You suspect me of some gross intent
Which this poor fellow rightly would resent?
D'you think me capable of such low acts?

CÉLIE

Ask him; he can support his charge with facts.

SGANARELLE

(To Célie:)
No, madam, pray speak on in my defense;
I couldn't match your force and eloquence.

Scene 22

Célie, Lélie, Sganarelle, Sganarelle's Wife, Célie's Maid.

WIFE

(To Célie:)
Madam, I shall not make a great to-do
And fly into a jealous rage at you;
But I'm no fool, and I see what's taking place:
Some passions, madam, are scandalous and base,
And you could have a loftier design
Than to seduce a heart that's rightly mine.

CÉLIE

Well, that confession of love was frank and clear.

SGANARELLE

(To his wife:)
Slut, who invited you to interfere?
She was defending me. You're jealous of her
Because you fear she'll lure away your lover.

CÉLIE

(To Sganarelle's Wife:)
Don't worry; he doesn't attract me—not one whit.
(Turning toward Lélie:)
So! All I said was true, you must admit.

LÉLIE

What can you mean?

MAID

Lord! When and how this mess
Is going to be untangled, I can't guess.
I've held my peace, and listened as best I could,
But the more I've heard, the less I've understood.
It's time for me to play the referee.
(She places herself between Lélie and Célie.)
Now, I'm going to ask some questions. Listen to me.
(To Lélie:)
You, sir: What is it you hold against this lady?

LÉLIE

That she's thrown me over, despite the vows she made me;
That, when her rumored nuptials brought me flying
Hither on wings of love, my heart denying
That all its trustful hopes could have miscarried,
I found, on reaching home, that she was married.

MAID

Married! To whom?

LÉLIE

(Pointing at Sganarelle:)
To him.

MAID

To him, you say?

LÉLIE

Yes, him!

MAID

Who said so?

LÉLIE

He did, this very day.

MAID

(To Sganarelle:)
Is that the truth?

SGANARELLE

I only said that I
Was married to my wife.

LÉLIE

You won't deny
That you had my portrait in your hands just now?

SGANARELLE

No. Here it is.

LÉLIE

And did you not avow
That you'd received it from a woman who
Was joined by matrimonial bonds to you?

SGANARELLE

(Pointing to his wife:)
Quite so. I snatched it from her, and learned thereby
What sins she was committing on the sly.

WIFE

Oh, stop these baseless accusations! I found
That locket, quite by chance, upon the ground;
(Pointing to Lélie:)

And later, when he had a dizzy fit
And I bade him come inside and rest a bit,
I didn't even connect him with that painting.

CÉLIE

I fear I started all of this, by fainting;
I dropped the portrait when I swooned, and he
(*Indicating Sganarelle:*)
Then carried me into the house most gallantly.

MAID

If I hadn't given you folks a little pill
Of common sense, you'd all be raving still.

SGANARELLE

(*Aside:*)
Is everything cleared up? It is, I guess.
But my brow felt hot for a while there, nonetheless.

WIFE

Not all my painful doubts have been relieved;
Though I'd like to trust you, I'd hate to be deceived.

SGANARELLE

Come, let's suppose each other to be true;
Since that's a greater risk for me than you,
You ought to find the bargain fair and square.

WIFE

All right. But if I catch you out, beware!

CÉLIE

(*To Lélie, they having been conversing in low voices:*)
Alas! In that case, what have I done? I dread

The fate to which my vengeful wrath has led.
I thought you faithless, and to give you ill
For ill, I bowed then to my father's will,
And have agreed just now to wed at last
A suitor I've discouraged in the past.
I've promised Father, and I'm afraid that he . . .
But I see him coming.

LÉLIE

He'll keep his word to me.

Scene 23

Gorgibus, Célie, Lélie, Sganarelle, Sganarelle's Wife, Célie's Maid.

LÉLIE

Sir, as you see, I'm back in town once more,
Full of a love as ardent as before,
And sure that, as you promised, you'll soon confer
Your daughter's hand on me, who worship her.

GORGIBUS

Sir, as I see, you're back in town once more,
Full of a love as ardent as before,
And sure that, as I promised, I'll soon confer
My daughter's hand on you, who worship her.
I am your lordship's humble servant, sir.

LÉLIE

Sir! Will you dash my hopes? Must I despair?

GORGIBUS

Sir, I but do my duty to Valère,
As will my daughter.

CÉLIE

My duty bids me, rather,
To keep the promise that you gave him, Father.

GORGIBUS

Is that what an obedient girl should say?
Do you forget that you agreed today
To marry Valère? . . . But I see his father heading
This way, perhaps to talk about the wedding.

Scene 24

Villebrequin, Gorgibus, Célie, Lélie, Sganarelle, Sganarelle's Wife, Célie's Maid.

GORGIBUS

Ah, my dear Villebrequin, what brings you here?

VILLEBREQUIN

A just-discovered secret which, I fear,
Will force me to go back on what I've said.
My son, whom your good daughter agreed to wed,
Has fooled us all: For four months, if you please,
He's covertly been married to Élise.
Since her family's rich, and she a brilliant catch,
I've no good reason to annul the match,
And so it seems—

GORGIBUS

No matter. For if Valère
Has made a marriage of which you weren't aware,
I must confess that, long ago, Célie
Was promised to this fine young man by me,

And that, since his return today, I've banned
All others from applying for her hand.

VILLEBREQUIN

An excellent choice.

LÉLIE

(To Gorgibus:)
       You've kept your word by this
Decision, sir, which fills my heart with bliss.

GORGIBUS

Let's go and plan the wedding.

SGANARELLE

(Alone:)
       It seemed so strong,
The evidence that my wife had done me wrong!
(To the audience:)
But as you've seen, in matters of this kind,
Appearances can deceive the keenest mind.
Remember my example, and be wise:
When things look simple, don't believe your eyes.

END OF PLAY

JEAN-BAPTISTE POQUELIN MOLIÈRE (1622–1673) was a French playwright and actor. Molière's plays include *The Misanthrope, Tartuffe, The School for Wives, The School for Husbands, The Miser, Lovers' Quarrels, The Imaginary Invalid* and *The Imaginary Cuckold, or Sganarelle,* among others.

RICHARD WILBUR is author of more than thirty-five books, including works of poetry, translation, prose, children's books and essays. Wilbur is the most prolific and gifted translator of Molière, and is credited with the explosive revival of Molière's plays in North America, beginning in 1955 with *The Misanthrope.* Wilbur's translations of Molière, Racine, Corneille and others are widely praised for incorporating the spirit of both language and author, while maintaining the original form and rhyme scheme. Wilbur is the only living American poet to have won the Pulitzer Prize twice. He has been awarded the National Book Award, the Bollingen Prize, two PEN translation awards and two Guggenheim fellowships. He served as U.S. Poet Laureate. Wilbur taught on the faculties of Harvard, Wellesley, Wesleyan and Smith (where he is poet emeritus). He lives in Cummington, Massachusetts, and is at present the Simpson Lecturer at Amherst College.